THE CAUSE GOES ON ...

THE CAUSE GOES ON …

REJOINING THE BATTLE TO MAKE AMERICA GREAT AGAIN

JUDGE HAL MOROZ

NEW YORK   ATLANTA   WASHINGTON   JERUSALEM

The Cause Goes On …

Rejoining the Battle to Make America Great Again

Judge Hal Moroz

Freedom is never more than one generation
away from extinction.
We didn't pass it to our children in the bloodstream.
It must be fought for, protected, and handed on for them to do
the same, or one day we will spend our sunset years telling
our children and our children's children what it was once like
in the United States where men were free.

~ President Ronald Reagan

This is the most important election
in the history of our country!

~ President Donald Trump

All to the Glory of God

The Cause Goes On ...

Contents

[Pictures of and with Judge Hal Moroz, pages 91 – 98]

Introduction

Fighting the Good Fight

You and I have a rendezvous with destiny. We will preserve for our children this, the last best hope of man on earth, or we will sentence them to take the first step into a thousand years of darkness.

If we fail, at least let our children and our children's children say of us we justified our brief moment here. We did all that could be done.

~ President Ronald Reagan

We are in a state of crisis. This is not hyperbole. America is at its most consequential election in the history of the republic. And the choices this election have never been clearer: Freedom or Tyranny, War or Peace, Order or Anarchy, Civility or Barbarism, Republican or Democrat, Good or Evil. These are the choices.

On one side of this presidential election, we have a challenger who placed at the top of his priority lists two warnings: (1) If people voted for him, their taxes would be raised; and (2) He would impose a three-month mandatory mask requirement for all citizens. The candidate is Joe Biden, whose claim to fame is a half-century in politics, making it clear his agenda would focus on empowering government, not citizens. And at his Democrat National Convention, Biden declared, "Silence is complicity!" He and his party then remained silent throughout their convention on the lawless violence and looting of his supporters on the streets of America's Democrat-run cities. And they removed God from the Pledge of Allegiance. In Conventions past, they even booed God. By his own testimony, Biden is complicit in the lawless, Godless anarchy of his supporters.

As President Trump so accurately pointed out in his address to the Republican National Convention on August 27, 2020, "This is the most important election in the history of our country!" He was right! It is! The Rule of Law is under attack! America is under attack!

Biden's agenda is one focusing on the ultimate abolition of private property. It is a vision heralded by Karl Marx more than a century ago, and its modern-day champions are found in the violent inner cities of America's Democrat-run strongholds.

Yet, as these same violent activists decry Capitalism and justify looting as a form of "reparations," they would kill if anyone took their smartphones or name-branded designer shoes or clothing. It is a brand of Marxism that is best summed up as: Marxism for thee, but not for me! They are the failed ideologies found in the BLM and so-called Antifa movements. Ignorant, violent and identified by their double-standards. They are what Jesus Christ called "Hypocrites." And these Marxists know this, and it is one of the many reasons they literally hate Christianity. They are as barbaric as the Islamic State fanatics and their caliphate that President Trump and the United States military destroyed, something eight years of Obama-Biden never did, or perhaps more accurately, never wanted to do. They coddled and emboldened terrorists, from dropping off planeloads of cash to the Ayatollahs in Iran to "trading" one American traitor for five Islamic war lords to return to the killing fields of the Middle East. The Obama-Biden administration was never about making America a shining city on a hill, it was about humbling America and bringing its citizen to their knees … something the professional sports franchises and their ungrateful prima donnas do with ever increasing regularity. They are an affront to the legions of Americans who fought and died throughout our noble history to preserve and protect the God-given rights and freedoms woven into the very fabric of our nation and the Constitution.

And even as the Obama-Biden regime lingered in its lame duck existence following the 2016 election, Obama, Biden and a group of conspirators sought to use America's intelligence apparatus and legal system to thwart and overturn the Constitutional mandate of America's voters. They spied on the fledgling Trump transition team and presidency, heralding one of the greatest abuses of power in our nation's history. The consequences of which are yet to be realized. But this event horizon will define our continued existence as a nation of laws, as our Founders envisioned, or a tyranny that no longer values the proposition of equal justice under the law and individual liberty.

This abuse of power and the need to restore our judiciary and respect for the rule of law were major reasons I entered the race for Justice on the Supreme Court of Georgia in March of 2020.

And in that race, the good people of Georgia spoke, and incumbent Justice Sarah Warren won, and she won decisively! But when all was said and done, 446,026 informed Georgians cast their votes for our campaign to support the cause we embraced for good government, and a rebirth of respect for our God-given Freedoms and Constitutional Rights. And millions nationwide were alerted to the problems facing our society and our judiciary. So all in all, it was a good race!

What I did discover in my race was a yearning for truth and a return to America's founding values and principles. And I was joined by old and new friends in my quest. Old friends like former Judge Kathe Loeffler, Chief Shannon Brock of the Watkinsville [Georgia] Police Department, Paul and Vickie Hafer, Martin Turner, and Steve Curtis of WECC Christian radio in St. Marys, Georgia, and Donna Fiducia and Don Neuen of Cowboy Logic Radio, Audrey Russo of the REEL Talk radio show, and concerned citizens like Rindy Howell of St. Marys and statesman and former Deputy

Assistant Secretary of the U.S. Army Van Hipp. And new friends like the Mayor of Valdosta [Georgia] and radio host, Scott James Matheson … and the list goes on and on, more than 446,000 new friends and informed voters, who knew who and what they were voting for. No man or campaign is a failure with friends such as these!

My greatest concern was always the thought of disappointing those who supported me. I hope I did not let them down or make them lose hope in our future. President Reagan said it best, when he declared in my youth, "America's best days are yet to come!" He was right! They are! Believe it! I believe in the promise of Romans 8:28.

And so there is no doubt, I lost my June 2020 race for Justice on the Supreme Court of Georgia, and I lost a great many other battles in my life, and I have lost loved ones, but *The Cause Goes On*! And I have come to realize that failure is sometimes the first step toward success. "Lay me down and bleed awhile," Reagan said in 1976, when he lost his first bid to become President and unseat an incumbent. "Though I am wounded, I am not slain." As the Great Communicator said, "I shall rise and fight again." He did!

The truth is: America is in the midst of a very troubling time. We no longer have a Constitutional system of checks and balances. Darkness has descended upon our country and has taken root in the Judiciary, starting in the United States Supreme Court and cascading down to our state courts, affecting even my beloved Georgia Supreme Court, where I have practiced the law with regularity. Our modern Judiciary has strayed from the narrowly defined role given it by the Framers, and has set out on a new progressive course, piloted by activist judges and justices, to divine laws that are anathema to the Constitution. It is a usurpation of the charter established by our Founding Fathers, and an affront to the God-given rights enumerated in our Constitution.

I say this as a concerned citizen who cares about the future of this republic, and I say this from a position of authority as a former judge and professor of law, as a prosecutor and as a bar member of the United States Supreme Court, who has practiced before the high Court, and many others.

We have descended into a nation with clearly defined battle lines, as stark and as clear as ever before, and I would include the Revolutionary and Civil War eras in this statement. The stakes were never higher, and the consequences never greater.

We now have federal judges actively opposing President Trump's plenary powers under the Constitution and substituting their notions on what the law should be. They have barred the President from banning travel to America by foreign nationals coming from countries with a history of hostility toward the United States and its citizens, and this is done in spite of Congressional statutes,[1] Executive Orders, and the Constitution giving the President express authority to ban such threats. These activist federal judges have ruled that protections afforded U.S. citizens under the Constitution shall

---

[1] 8 U.S. Code § 1182.

be extended to non-citizen foreigners in caravans outside of our country traveling north to our southern border with Mexico. They have even perverted the 14th Amendment, which was designed to give citizenship to slaves, to somehow apply to illegal trespassers who give birth on American soil. Their rationale is that these so-called "anchor babies" are protected as citizens by the 14th Amendment, totally ignoring that these are non-citizens, who are subject to the jurisdiction of their home countries. These are edicts by unelected judges that have no basis in law, but the Congress is unwilling to intervene and stop this perversion of the Constitution and, thereby, check the Judiciary. These non-citizens, like foreign diplomats, are the subjects of foreign powers, only these foreigners are here illegally. The 14th Amendment was never intended to give license to criminal acts.[2] We even have judges ordering the return of foreign criminals deported from the United States for their lawlessness back to the United States, in violation of state and federal laws prohibiting such actions. These are gross violations of the role established for our judges and justices in legal precedent and codified law. This is a Constitutional crisis.

If Joe Biden had his way, America would be a borderless sanctuary for illegals, and the recipient of unchecked Communist Chinese carriers of the plague that ravaged the world. Thank God President Trump had the wisdom and the

---

[2] The 14th Amendment to the U.S. Constitution was adopted on July 9, 1868: "All persons born or naturalized in the United States, and subject to the jurisdiction thereof, are citizens of the United States and of the state wherein they reside. No state shall make or enforce any law which shall abridge the privileges or immunities of citizens of the United States; nor shall any state deprive any person of life, liberty, or property, without due process of law; nor deny to any person within its jurisdiction the equal protection of the laws."

vision to build the wall on our southern border and ban travel from mainland China, both, by the way, over the strong vocal objection of Joe Biden, Nancy Pelosi, and Chuck Schumer, who accused the President of being a "fear-monger and xenophobe!" How wrong these Democrats were, and how right the President was and continues to be!

Since Donald Trump's initial nomination for President in 2016, the Democrats, led by Obama, Biden, and a cabal of conspirators in the Deep State bowels of our government, have gone out of their way to use every method, legal and otherwise, to derail the agenda of our President and blunt America's return to greatness. From illegally spying on the President-elect to concocting a false narrative to execute a coup under the guise of an impeachment, Democrats have irreparably harmed America ... but all is not lost, and the cause goes on!

This book provides answers to our problems, and contains the Founding Documents of our country, which include the Declaration of Independence, the Federalist Papers, and the Supreme Law of the Land: The U.S. Constitution, so you can refer to the principles I cite. These are the blueprints for America's return to greatness, and form the bulk of ideas and principles upon which our nation was founded and must return to if we are to endure and prosper.

These documents are not great mysteries, as the media pundits and legal profession would have you believe. The Bible says its authors were holy men of old who spoke as God the Holy Spirit moved them.[3] I believe such can also be said of our Founders. Our Founding Documents extoll the principles upon which our nation was founded, and the role of our state and federal governments. In the final analysis, these documents and this book embody a plan to reclaim America's Founding Principles and greatness.

In a nutshell, We the People must ensure that all who would serve in government strictly interpret the Constitution as the Founders intended, and not substitute their will for the Law. The success of this experiment in republican government depends on this adherence to that Founding Principle. Our future generations will reap the rewards or suffer the consequences of the choices we now make on electing our political leaders, including seating judges and justices in the Judiciary. Let us decide well, having the knowledge and the wisdom to choose wisely. As President Trump said, "This is the most important election in the history of our country!"

~ Judge Hal Moroz

---

[3] 2 Peter 1:21, KJV: "For the prophesy came not in old time by the will of man: but holy men of God spake as they were moved by the Holy Ghost."

A wise man will hear, and will increase learning;
and a man of understanding shall attain unto wise counsels:
To understand a proverb, and the interpretation;
the words of the wise, and their dark sayings.

~ Proverbs 1:5-6

Chapter 1

Our Hour of Action

There should be no fear! We are protected, and we will always be protected! We will be protected by the great men and women of our military and law enforcement and, most importantly, we are protected by God!

Now arrives the hour of action! Do not let anyone tell you it cannot be done! No challenge can match the heart and fight and spirit of America! We will not fail! Our country will thrive and prosper again!

~ President Donald J. Trump,
January 20, 2017

When I became a lawyer, I was given a ring. I wear it still. The ring is a simple band of gold, inscribed with a Latin maxim, "Lex Est Arma Regum," meaning, "Law is the Arm of the King." The ring was commissioned by King James of England—the same King James who commissioned the 1611

King James Version of the Holy Bible. The bearers of these rings were the representative arms of the law and the King. The ring was historically bestowed on knights of the realm who served the cause of justice, law and order. It was part of an oath to support and defend the law. Bestowed upon these trusted knights was the right to bear arms, and the power to meet justice. They maintained a duty and a trust that endures even to the present day.

I wrote and compiled this book to honor our country, the Law, and the legions of brave young Americans who fought and died to preserve our republic and defend its Constitution. The Supreme Court broke trust with the Constitution and the people of America, who appointed and confirmed each justice to the high Court through our elected representatives. And I present this work as a former soldier who served this country, and as a lawyer, educator, prosecutor, and a former judge. I speak as a citizen here, having a constitutional right to the freedom of speech, and I do so for the purpose of promoting the kind of grassroots change that can restore the Supreme Court and our lower courts, and our constitutional system of checks and balances.

We surrendered many of our God-given Freedoms and Constitutional Rights in the first months of the COVID-19 pandemic. Without a shot being fired, Americans accepted being ordered to "shelter in place," that is, submit to house arrest. And we were not under charge for any crime or diagnosed as being sick. We were ordered NOT to attend church, because doing so would subject those seeking to practice their Christian faith to arrest. This was a direct violation of the Constitution, as the First Amendment guarantees every citizen that the government "shall make no law" that "prohibits the free exercise" of our religion. Yet like sheep we followed the dictates of the government, that lacked the Constitutional authority to issue such edicts. And barely a word was spoken in opposition, especially by our Judiciary. I spoke about this at length in an interview on The Lighthouse WECC radio, which can be found on YouTube at "Hal Moroz for Georgia Supreme Court – The Lighthouse WECC Interview" and on my website at MorozLaw.com. But this state of affairs was years in the making.

Marbury v. Madison[4] was the landmark Supreme Court case that established the doctrine of Judicial Review and set in stone the role of judges and justices in our Constitutional system of checks and balances. Judges and justices are there to interpret the law as written, not make up law. Their duty is to ensure the Constitution is upheld, not usurped.

However, on June 25, 2015, the Supreme Court broke trust with that precedent, the United States Constitution, and We the People of America! In *King v. Burwell*, the Supreme Court changed the express words of the legislation passed by the U.S. Congress, and substituted their will for the Law.

The very next day, in *Obergefell v. Hodges*, the Supreme Court again broke trust and usurped the Constitutional jurisdiction of the states and the people, and rewrote 5,000 years of an established definition of marriage and fabricated

---

[4] *Marbury v. Madison*, 5 U.S. 137 (1803).

Constitutional protections for a deviant class it supported.

In the words of the late, great Justice Antonin Scalia in his *Obergefell* dissent, "This is a naked judicial claim to legislative — indeed, super-legislative — power; a claim fundamentally at odds with our system of government...A system of government that makes the People subordinate to a committee of nine unelected lawyers does not deserve to be called a democracy."

The primary purpose of this book, *The Cause Goes On*, is to serve as a wakeup call about the critical nature of the 2020 Election and the Constitutionally established role of our citizens – You and me – in keeping our republic. We have a duty to actually know the policies of those we elect to the Presidency and the Congress, and, at the state-level, our governors, legislators, judges, mayors and city council members, to name a few. Our votes for statesmen and women to these cherished institutions are vital to the survival of our republic!

Making America Great Again requires a commitment to the cause, and the embodiment of the same mindset and work ethic that made America great to begin with. Truth, Justice, a reverence to God and our country's Founding Principles, and the vision and good deeds to see them through. This includes voting for the re-election of President Trump, a Conservative-Republican Congress, and state-level champions of America's Founding Principles, whether they be governors, judges, legislators, mayors, school board members or city council members. Re-electing President Trump at the national level and electing patriots like Marjorie Taylor Greene to Congress in northwest Georgia and Rindy Howell to the St. Marys City Council at the local level in Georgia and elsewhere is what *The Cause Goes On* is all about!

Under our Constitution, the government exists to perform a well-defined function. It is NOT the master of We the People, and it was designed to be manned by public servants in our republican form of government. The Judiciary, for example, does not exist to make laws and impose its will on We the People. But, unfortunately, our modern Judiciary has strayed from that narrowly defined role, and has set out on a new progressive course, piloted by activist judges and justices, to divine laws that are anathema to the Constitution. It is a usurpation of the charter established by our Founding Fathers, and an affront to the God-given rights enumerated in our Constitution. It is a Constitutional crisis.

I have a vision of what our Judiciary should be, based on my understanding of the Constitution and our Founding Principles as a nation. And having a vision is important. In Proverbs 29:18, we read, "Where there is no vision, the people perish: but he that keepeth the law, happy is he." When William F. Buckley, Jr., ran for mayor of the city of my youth, he ran against a liberal, John V. Lindsay, and lost. That was in 1965, and a year later, Buckley wrote a book, *The Unmaking of a Mayor*. He lost the battle, but ultimately won the war. Through his outspoken, sometimes unpopular, championship of conservative principles, Buckley breathed life into ideas as old as the republic, in a society that was overwhelmed by a liberal, politically correct philosophy. His was a voice on a vision that cried out in the wilderness, and millions of Americans, including yours truly, heard the call. Bill Buckley set the stage for the election of his younger brother, and one of my political heroes, James L. Buckley, to become the Conservative U.S. Senator from the State of New York following his election in 1970. And, more importantly, Buckley created a movement from a vision that culminated in the elections of Ronald Reagan in 1980 and Donald Trump in 2016.

I believe each of us in our own way has a role to play in the betterment of our society. We have good works to do. As I often told members of juries in felony cases I prosecuted for the State of Georgia as an Assistant District Attorney, "The only thing necessary for the triumph of evil is for good men to do nothing." It was a quote from Edmund Burke, an eighteenth century philosopher who criticized British treatment of the American colonies, and championed the virtues of good manners in society and the importance of the Christian church as a moral stabilizing influence in the state. Burke is considered the founder of the modern Conservative movement.

Being a judge is a great honor and a distinct privilege, whether on the state or federal level. It is also a unique experience, which entails great responsibility. It is quite different from the role of an advocate, although the two serve as officers of the court. A judge, unlike a lawyer, cannot be an advocate for either party in the courtroom. Decisions are made based on the facts and the law. The judge or the justice is the gatekeeper, the articulator of the Law, and a sworn defender of the Constitution, as written.

However, with the precedent set by the Roberts Supreme Court in *Obergefell v. Hodges* and *King v. Burwell*, judges are no longer confined to that ideal, and instead have been given licenses to rewrite the laws of the legislature and substitute their will for the law. The Roberts Supreme Court, I predict, will go down in history with the same negative connotations applied to the Supreme Court of the *Scott v. Sandford* decision more than a century and a half ago, but for difference reasons.

In reality, the *Dred Scott*[5] decision upheld the express words of the Constitution and the letter of the Law, but was vilified in the North for being out of step with the abolitionist movement. The decision actually addressed the legal standing of a petitioner to file suit based on the facts and the law. It highlighted the need for legislative action.

Despite it fueling the North's vilification of the Taney[6] Court at the time, the decision kept faith with the Constitution and the duty of the Supreme Court in the constitutional framework of our republic. That role is found in the Constitution and was established by the Supreme Court in its landmark 1803 *Marbury v. Madison* opinion. As Hamilton proclaimed in *The Federalist No. 78*, "The courts must declare the sense of the law; and if they should be disposed to exercise WILL instead of JUDGMENT, the consequence would be the substitution of their pleasure to that of the legislative body."

---

[5] *Dred Scott v. Sandford*, 60 U.S. 393 (1857), was a landmark opinion by the U.S. Supreme Court that held that immigrants who entered America as slaves and their descendants were not U.S citizens under the Constitution, and therefore had no standing in federal court to file lawsuits.
[6] Chief Justice Roger B. Taney.

But even with this clear admonishment from a Founding Father, the Supreme Court has dramatically strayed from its Founding Principles, and there rages a great debate in the modern judiciary. Judges are divided on the limits of their power and their roles on the bench. Many of the Liberal persuasion believe their job is to interpret the law in an innovative fashion, even creating laws at times, to dispense a brand of justice that suits popular opinion or their own good pleasure. It is the type of jurisprudence that was exercised by the United States Supreme Court in 2015, and by the Florida Supreme Court in 2000 in *Gore v. Bush*.

Barack Hussein Obama did manage to keep one of his campaign promises of 2008: he fundamentally transformed America! Who would have believed that less than two decades after the 9/11 attacks on America that we would now be a nation on the brink of welcoming tens of thousands Muslim so-called "refugees" into this shining city on a hill. We have even elected them to the U.S. Congress. These "refugees," predominantly military-age men, are surging through Europe and headed toward America. And these hordes have already left a path of destruction in their wake. The scene is reminiscent of the state of affairs that beset Rome some 1500 years ago.

Even more alarming, as I write these words, millions of illegal immigrants are roaming the streets of America in violation of federal and state law, and they now have the blessing of the mainstream media and activist judges to remain in this land and take advantage of our legal safeguards and safety nets which were originally designed for legal citizens. These include privileges of free healthcare, welfare, immunity granted by sanctuary cities, and freedom to vote in any election without the benefit of having to prove who they are. While identification cards are required to receive access to the most basic resources in our society, illegal aliens, with the blessing of our courts, need not identify themselves through the production of an identification card in order to vote. California even issues them Drivers Licenses and the privilege to vote. The consequences of these foolish acts are destructive to our culture. This invites the creation of an electorate and a system of government that is controlled by a plurality of noncitizens motivated to vote by their benefactors who prey on their desire to receive free benefits in return for keeping their enablers in office via the vote. It is a state of affairs our Founding Fathers warned us about in the early days of our republic. It is self-destructive!

To combat the inevitable demise of the republic by these edicts, a vocal and growing movement has emerged. This is the Movement championed by President Trump.

This can be seen clearly in the 2016 presidential race. Americans are soundly rejecting the established politicians who reside in all three branches of government, and here I most certainly include the judiciary.

I disagree with Judicial Activism. I consider it a threat to the Constitution and our republic. And it is most certainly a breach of the oaths to the Constitution and the Judicial Cannons that judges and justices take and must abide by. I hold to the Conservative proposition that all American courts adhere to the strict interpretation of the Constitution and be consistent with the original intent of our Founding Fathers. It is emphatically the province and duty of the judiciary to say what the law is, not what it should be. If judges want to make laws, let them run for legislative office. Judges are there to interpret the law, nothing more and nothing less. And that in itself is an awesome task. And this is the reason for this work: To explain the substance and role of a member of the government, including the Judiciary, so We the People of the United States can make an informed and wise decision about the executive officers we elect to appoint judges and justices, as well as the judges and justices we directly elect. These are critical decisions affecting the future of our children and the continuing existence of the republic. This is our role in combating evil in our time!

Judges hold positions of great trust and power. The latter must be exercised wisely, using great restraint, and with exceeding sound judgment. To wield that sword to satisfy his or her personal whims or desires, I believe, is a breach of duty and the public trust placed in that individual, and an act which is in diametrical opposition to the intent of our Founding Fathers when they established the Judiciary under our Constitution.

Justice Benjamin Cardozo said it best in 1921, when he addressed the debate in its formative stages during his time:

> The Judge, even when he is free, is still not
> wholly free. He is not to innovate at pleasure. He

is not a knight-errant, roaming at will in pursuit of his own ideal of beauty or of goodness. He is to draw his inspiration from consecrated principles. He is not to yield to spasmodic sentiment, to vague and unregulated benevolence. He is to exercise a discretion informed by tradition, methodized by analogy, disciplined by system, and subordinated to "the primordial necessity of order in the social life." Wide enough in all conscience is the field of discretion that remains.

The year 2015 marked a turning point for the judiciary in America. The Supreme Court of the United States violated the Constitution in two back-to-back decisions. In its June *King v. Burwell* decision, six of the nine justices on the Supreme Court substituted their will for the will of the Congress, and enabled the implementation of ObamaCare to proceed. These justices became lawmakers by substituting the words of the Congress for their own words in violation of their duty to the Constitution and the people of the United States of America. They violated a sacred trust!

As I recently mentioned to friends who serve as judges, the Supreme Court has made it impossible for me to teach civil procedure in good conscience. The activist justices have turned the process for deciding cases on its head. They no longer rely on precedent or subscribe to the principles espoused in *Marbury* and codified in the Constitution. They have become a law unto themselves.

In *Obergefell v. Hodges*, the Supreme Court rewrote more than 5000 years of established marital relations, and gave a new definition to marriage. They did this by manufacturing a connection between the homosexual lifestyle and the protections afforded American citizens under the Constitution. A razor-thin majority (five out of the nine justices) on the Court substituted their will for the Law and usurped the Constitution, in a manner much like they justified the barbaric murder of millions of unborn American citizens through abortion. In *Roe v. Wade*,[7] the Court expanded the notion of "privacy" to such an extent as to allow mothers to be exploited by abortionists and baby parts sellers to actually kill their babies. And the Court did this without regard to the constitutional protections of the babies under the Fifth Amendment to the Constitution, which states, "No person shall be…deprived of life, liberty, or property, without due process of law."

I believe Life begins at conception, and science supports that proposition, especially since the days of *Roe v. Wade*. Nevertheless, the topic of Abortion is political, but the issue of Life and the Law in America is fixed by our Constitution. Life is protected under the Constitution. Life is an enumerated God-given right under our Constitution, which cannot be extinguished without Due Process. Abortion on demand is unconstitutional and a violation of the rights of our most vulnerable citizens, our unborn living children. I find it fascinating that our scientific community searches for "life" on other planets through the exploration of microscopic

---

[7] *Roe v. Wade*, 410 U.S. 113 (1973).

organisms, but shies away from the notion that an 8 month old fetus in his or her mother's womb, with a heartbeat and emotions and dreams and all the features of a gendered human being, could possibly be a "life." To call such a baby anything other than a human life, a citizen deserving of protection under the Law, is unreasonable.

These millions of aborted babies since the high Court's decision in *Roe* were most certainly deprived of life and liberty. It is a national disgrace and a level of barbarism rivalling Nazi Germany, Communist powers like China and the old Soviet Union, and Islam. It is my hope in the years to come that America will investigate these butchers who kill these babies and profit from the sale of their body parts. There is no statute of limitations on murder, and if murder and other violations of law were committed, they should and must be prosecuted. The excuse of "I was only following orders" or "It was acceptable under [Nazi] law to do so" will not be an adequate excuse or legal defense. Our Constitution speaks otherwise.

Literally minutes after the *Obergefell* decision, I was on "The Lighthouse" WECC Christian Radio (TheLighthouseFM.org) with its president, Paul Hafer, sharing my views on the unprecedented move by the Supreme Court to redefine marriage, which is specifically in the jurisdiction of the states, and aid Obama in his radical transformation of America and Western Civilization. The Constitution was being dismantled before our very eyes. The high Court was aiding the Executive Branch in usurping the Constitution, and the Republican-led

Congress was disavowing its sworn duty and its multiple campaign promises to the American people to stop it.

For the first time in my life, as I drove home from the court on that fateful Friday in June 2015, I seriously wondered, what good is a Supreme Court that forsakes its duty under the Constitution to support the tyrannical agenda of a chief executive, in this case, Barack Hussein Obama?

The unprecedented rise of outsiders to the political process like Donald Trump and others is evidence of the broad-based rejection by the American people of politics as usual. And fueling this rejection is the conduct of so-called "opposition-party" leaders in the GOP. These men were given a mandate and control of the American Congress to oppose the fundamentally flawed transformational agenda of Barack Hussein Obama. They utterly failed, and in many instances, enabled that destructive agenda to succeed. It was a betrayal of the sacred trust bestowed upon these men and women by the American people.

On issue after issue, be it ObamaCare or the treaty with Iran masquerading as an executive deal by Obama, the Republican leadership in Congress and the Judiciary failed the American people and the system of checks and balances guaranteed in the Constitution and the ruling in *Marbury*.

A consequence of Barack Hussein Obama's fundamental transformation of America includes the death of the great American Spirit. This can be seen in a mindset that doubts America's exceptionalism. This is manifest in a multitude of naysayers who believe the construction of a great wall along the border with Mexico, the deportation of millions of illegal criminals, and the repeal and replacement of ObamaCare with an affordable and exceptional healthcare system is "impossible." And this is said in a country that has been endowed by God with the ability to do the impossible. We survived and prospered after a horrific civil war that pit brother against brother, went on to win two world wars, cured many of the so-called incurable diseases, and landed men on the moon and returned them safely to the earth.

With all the exceptional things America has accomplished, like building the Panama Canal through the Western Hemisphere, providing emergency relief and medicine to the world, and being a beacon of hope, just to name a few, I am stunned by the doubters. We actually have citizens, and men and women aspiring to the highest office in the land, saying America can no longer do great things! How very sad.

If this book has any message, it is this: America's Constitutional system is broken, but it is not beyond repair. In fact, it can be made stronger and greater than ever before, but it will take the concerted efforts of individual citizens to restore the building blocks of our republic. And a vital building block of our republic is the Presidency, and the men and women we choose to stand watch on her walls. President Trump is the man for this moment!

Unfortunately, past presidents and the United States Supreme Court broke trust with the American people and violated its duty under the Constitution. The states have this problem as well. Many of our governors, mayors, and courts, by definition, have become lawless. But we can change this lawlessness, and it begins with a respect for the Constitution and the rule of law, and by understanding the role of those who would serve as elected officials, including judges and justices.

The Supreme Court and the Congress have unique Constitutional roles in placing a President's great power in check, and they effectively did so before the advent of activist judges and establishment politicians. These politicians found it personally advantageous to go along with or oppose whatever the chief executive proposes, ignoring the intent and constraints of our Constitution.

It is important to note a few things about Congress, despite what the current leadership may say. Congress exists as a co-equal branch of government with the Executive and the Judicial. It is responsible for making the laws. It is as important as the Executive and Judicial Branches in the scheme of the Constitution. And although more than 11,000 people, most of who were men, have served in both the House and Senate of the Congress since the signing of the Constitution, each member has a critical role to play in our republic. Consequently, the American public has a vital duty to fulfill when it votes for any candidate to hold an office of such high public trust.

President Donald J. Trump made the appointments of a new generation of judges and justices to the federal Judiciary --- some 300 to date --- with two of them serving on the United

States Supreme Court, and the Republican-led United States Senate confirmed them. It is imperative we replace the liberal activist justices, like Ginsburg, Beyer, Sotomayor and Kagan, with strict constitutionalists in the mold of Scalia, Thomas and Alito. I find Chief Justice Roberts an opportunist who straddles the fence that divides the judiciary, often venturing into activism, as he did in the ObamaCare decision and *King v. Burwell*. The Roberts Court is a hotbed of judicial activists, and their alliance with the radical Left must be thwarted. This is a time of choosing!

As the Democrat Party has failed to differentiate itself from the far-Left Socialist wing of the political spectrum, and having ostracized its Conservative remnants years ago, electing Conservative Republicans is the only logical means to preserving this Constitutional republic and restoring our Judiciary.

I pray we choose wisely, to preserve what Presidents Lincoln and Reagan called "this last best hope for man on earth." Our duty requires no more, and our posterity deserves no less than the America we inherited. This is keeping faith with the Constitution, and a very American thing to do!

Freedom is never more than one generation away from extinction. We didn't pass it to our children in the bloodstream. It must be fought for, protected, and handed on for them to do the same, or one day we will spend our sunset years telling our children and our children's children what it was once like in the United States where men were free.

~ President Ronald Reagan

Chapter 2

A Republic, If You Can Keep It

We have been assured, sir, in the sacred writings, that "except the Lord build the house they labor in vain that build it." I firmly believe this; and I also believe that without His concurring aid we shall succeed in this political building no better than the builders of Babel; we shall be divided by our little partial, local interests, our projects will be confounded and we ourselves shall become a reproach and a byword down to future ages. And, what is worse, mankind may hereafter, from this unfortunate instance, despair of establishing government by human wisdom and leave it to chance, war, or conquest.

Only a virtuous people are capable of freedom. As nations become more corrupt and vicious, they have more need of masters.

~ Benjamin Franklin

At the conclusion of America's Constitutional Convention of 1787, as the delegates exited Independence Hall, an anxious crowd gathered, wondering what the Founders had envisioned for the fledgling United States of America. A prominent socialite of the day, a Mrs. Powel of Philadelphia, caught the attention of Benjamin Franklin and asked, "Well, Doctor, what have we got, a republic or a monarchy?" Without hesitation, Franklin answered, "A republic, if you can keep it."

The question of whether or not this Republic can endure has been posed many times by many sources, but none so often and by as many as today. The Civil War, the assassination of several presidents, the scandals of yesteryear, Vietnam ~ all pale in comparison to the challenges we now face in preserving this "last best hope for man on earth," as President Reagan called her.

I spoke about this moment in history on a radio talk show hosted by my friend, Von Goodwin, in July of 2015. I shared my thoughts and views on the state of the union, and Von suggested my views, which were consistent with the birth of America, seemed somewhat prosaic and out of the mainstream. He nevertheless suggested that these ideas needed attention perhaps more now than ever before in our history as a republic. After much thought, I agree.

We are at a crossroads in America! One road leads to a continued republic, and the other to a dictatorship. The choice of which path we follow is still ours, but we are certainly running out of time to make that decision on our own. We stand at a precipice. America, for a variety of reasons we shall address, has been weakened at home and abroad, perhaps a better word would be crippled. The power America once projected as a moral leader and proponent for good around the globe appears to have come to an end. The sun is setting on this shining city on a hill. The light we once projected has dimmed, and at risk of going out.

You could say my idea for writing this book came amidst the 2016 presidential election campaign. Among the contenders were Democrats and Republicans. Philosophically, I am a Conservative and I have historically voted for the most Conservative Republican in every election since 1976, when I cast my first vote for Ronald Reagan to defeat a sitting incumbent president, Gerald R. Ford, for the Republican nomination.

President Reagan was my ideal of a statesman and American patriot. He embodied the Founding Principles I had come to embrace and articulate in my own life. His philosophy was simple: American government was based on our Founding document, the Constitution. This meant government had limited duties and powers, which were enunciated in that founding document, such as, providing for the common defense.

President Reagan understood that the primary responsibility of the government was to provide for the safety of its citizens. This is why we have a standing army, secured borders, local police and firefighters, courts, and the

Constitution itself. Out of this controlling principle, the federal government had its responsibilities and the states had theirs. Whatever was not the dominion of the federal government as articulated in the Constitution was reserved to the states and We the People. This embodies the principle of federalism, which is codified in the 10th Amendment to the Constitution.

However, today, some 40-plus years after I first voted, that philosophy of limited government and the notion that Americans could control their own destiny is lost. We now find the vast majority of Americans have lost faith with a system that they rightly feel has betrayed them.

In the past decade, America has gone through a radical transformation. This is no exaggeration. But we can say we are better off today than we were four short years ago. And we can thank President Trump for that! He successfully reversed the rising time of regulations and taxes, a weakened and demoralized military, American embassies sacked and our Ambassador killed under the Obama-Biden administration [for the first time since the Carter Administration], the finest healthcare system in the world dismantled to fulfill the dream of a socialist in the White House [Obama] and his allies in the Congress, illegal immigrants running unchecked across our borders and corrupting our culture, America's standing in the world diminished, and the list goes on and on. President Trump is fighting the good fight to return America to greatness.

At a time in our history when the great and noble deeds of our last generation freed a world from the tyranny of communism, we find a new emergence of that bankrupt philosophy in the very seat of our national government, with Chuck Schumer and Nancy Pelosi now leading the charge … and the obstruction to positive change! And there are many on the sidelines preparing to carry that corrupt banner, amongst whom we find the Democrat Party and their allies in the mainstream media.

Would my father, who died a month before the assassination of President Kennedy in 1963, even recognize the America of today if he were alive? Or for that matter, does the America of today even resemble the America that existed during the administration of President Reagan? Sadly, I think not to both. We are not better off than we were twelve, or thirty, or 100 years ago for that matter. But President Trump has improved America's standing in the last four years!

The Democrats have effectively tipped the scales in the electoral process to their dependents in this new age welfare state. And now they seek to remove any requirement for voters to positively identify themselves, effectively opening the door to voter fraud and giving illegal immigrants the right to vote.

Despite the best efforts of President Reagan and those of us who proudly participated in the Reagan Revolution, Americans have turned their backs on the core principles which made us a great nation. We failed to institutionalize the Conservative changes of the Reagan Revolution, and their popularity waned. Led by Obama and his cohorts, the Liberal Establishment and their champions in the Judiciary and the mainstream media, quietly dismantled our foundational pillars. They held the Constitution and the Holy Bible in contempt, and effectively rewrote the noble history of the United States in our public classrooms and institutions of "Higher Education." As Obama declared, "We are no longer a Christian nation!"

Like President Reagan, who often declared, "America's best days are yet to come," I still believe there is hope. That is why I voted for Donald J. Trump to become President and supported his Movement to Make America Great Again. And I will vote for President Trump again this year! But I understand that that is not enough. You and I must now follow through and actively support the agenda to truly Make America Great Again!

I make known to my friends and associates and representatives in government that I support the Conservative agenda of President Trump, and I pray for America every day, and work to make the hope of that prayer a reality. As long as we have Americans of faith standing in the gap for this "last best hope for man on earth," there is hope that we can overcome this prolonged transformation of America by the Left.

We might be approaching the biblical cities of Sodom and Gomorrah, but we are not there yet. Not by a long shot, not on our watch, and definitely not as long as we still have young Americans standing watch on the walls of this bright shining city on a hill.

It's Morning Again in America! We have a brief opportunity to make America great again, but as I said before, that will take We the People ensuring that all who would serve in the Executive, Legislative and Judiciary in our state and federal governments strictly interpret the Constitution as the Founders intended, and not substitute their will for the Law. Again, this would be a very American thing to do!

If my people, which are called by my name, shall humble themselves, and pray, and seek my face, and turn from their wicked ways; then will I hear from heaven, and will forgive their sin, and will heal their land.

~ 2 Chronicles 7:14

In a time when evil and darkness seems to prevail, Christ tells us once again, "Fear not!"

~ Pope John Paul II

Chapter 3

God and Country

God presides over the destinies of nations.

~ Patrick Henry

It is the duty of all Nations to acknowledge the providence of Almighty God.

~ President George Washington,
First Presidential Proclamation, October 3, 1789

America was founded by people who believe[d] that God was their rock of safety. I recognize we must be cautious in claiming that God is on our side, but I think it's all right to keep asking if we're on His side. The time has come to turn to God and reassert our trust in Him for the healing of America...Our country is in need of and ready for a spiritual renewal.

~ President Ronald Reagan

It is hard to argue that the protective hand of God has not been on America. From our very birth as a nation, we have done what no other people ever did in the history of man. We were the first to gain independence from the Crown on the simple proposition that men are "endowed by their Creator with certain unalienable Rights, that among these are Life, Liberty and the pursuit of Happiness—That to secure these rights, governments are instituted among men, deriving their just power from the consent of the governed." It was indeed revolutionary, and we succeeded!

We have since led the world in justice, technology, scientific discovery, humanitarian outreach, tolerance of religion—you name the noble cause, and America has been there! One of the undeniable truths in this country is the faith of our Founding Fathers. They were men of God, who acted upon their beliefs. The fact we are a nation built upon a Christian heritage is undeniable! This fact is evident in the Declaration of Independence, the Constitution, and virtually every document of American historical substance. Seals on licenses, commissions and other official documents refer to "the year of our Lord." Even our money bears the motto, "In God We Trust." Our state and national legislatures and courts all refer to God at one time or another during session. Our Congress begins each day with an opening prayer. Examples abound!

Nevertheless, our Christian heritage and traditions are under attack. We are bombarded by attacks from the Left to quash any reference to God in our daily lives. Democrats seek to "Cancel" our culture! But for what purpose, and to what end?

Throughout our country, we have attacks on America's Founders and core values, statutory displays of our historical figures and the Ten Commandments and prayer in public places (not Islamic chanting, mind you), and classes that teach good citizenship. But the battlefront does not end there. Even reference to the Ten Commandments is under assault in our nation's courtrooms. Imagine that! Simple nativity scenes in our local communities during Christmas time are openly, and many times successfully, challenged in courtrooms across the land. And the list goes on and on. What is amazing, however, is not the fact people object to any reference of God. The amazing thing is that we have people in responsible positions willing to entertain and support such agendas, and, unfortunately, many of them are sitting legislators and judges. Think about it!

In just this past decade, the Supreme Court of the United States has taken it upon itself to redefine marriage to accommodate a vocal minority that sought not so much to achieve "equal rights under the law," as they stated, but to destroy an institution (Marriage) that was defined by God and embraced by civilizations for thousands of years.

During what has been called the Greatest Generation, that

is, the World War II generation of my father, the thought of American lawyers, judges and justices, Congressman and Senators rallying to the aid of terrorists being treated "inhumanely" in the Caribbean while American soldiers were fighting and dying abroad would have been unthinkable! But, alas, this is a new day! We have judges and justices ruling against an elected president they despise, and advocating for the so-called "constitutional rights" of foreigners, illegal trespassers, and those who invade our country. Incredible! They give aid and comfort to the enemy.

Islam in its purest form proclaims itself incompatible with Western Civilization. Why are we disputing it? Better yet, why are our established political leaders in Washington denying it? And why are our judges and justices supporting this philosophy, which is anathema to our Constitution and our culture?

I realize such statements are controversial. Throughout my many years as both a student and a teacher, I have heard the old adage of never mix religion with politics. I have come to discover the complete lack of wisdom in that proposition. Politics is a struggle between ideas. What greater struggle exists in our day and age than that which can be found in the war of religious ideas? For Christians, that struggle is found in the spiritual realm. We follow the dictates of Holy Scripture, the foremost of which is the teaching of Jesus Christ. It is a religion of peace and good will.

Islam, on the other hand, is a political movement masquerading as a religion. It is a fanatical movement steeped in violence, intolerance, and the eradication of the infidel. Unfortunately for Christians, we are the infidels, along with our Jewish brethren. It is not a movement of coexistence. And it is an existential threat to the American way of life, the West, and all of Christendom. This is not my opinion, it is an historical fact. And we can ignore it at our own peril, or in the words of Shakespeare, we can take arms against the struggle and by opposing, end it! This was the central meaning of the Crusades. They were a great force for good that confronted evil in their time, defeated it, and ended what was known as the Dark Ages.

We as a nation and as a people of Western Civilization would do well to remember the lessons of the Crusades. When evil is confronted, it is stopped. When good men do nothing in the face of evil, evil triumphs.

I appreciate the fact President Trump is building a great wall along our southern border, and wants to deport illegal criminals and the jihadist "refugees" Obama welcomed to America, end ObamaCare, stop the persecution of Christians, and recognize that the government is a servant of the people, and not their master.

However, this America First agenda is under fire by the Liberal mainstream media and others who should know better. But the more President Trump speaks of these issues, the more popular he becomes, and the greater the threat he poses to the establishment that prefer the status quo. President Trump quickly became the target of their personal attacks. These attacks were formalized in illegal spying and lying to courts by operatives in the Obama-Biden administration, and the appointment of a Special Prosecutor with unconstitutional, unchecked "authority" and limitless jurisdiction to pursue Donald Trump in the hopes of discovering a crime in his past. This is anathema to the Constitutional notions of a presumption of innocence and due process. The idea here is: if you can kill the messenger, you kill the message! It is not consistent with our system of Justice.

In today's world, we have every right to be sceptical, especially when we look at the current Congressional leadership. These were men and women who were given majorities to stop the creeping cancer of Socialism, and not only failed to stop it but wound up enabling it. Some question President Trump's sincerity as a populist Conservative. I do not, and I believe people can learn and grow and change their minds on certain issues. That's a part of life. But I do abhor politicians who make promises knowing full well they never meant to keep them. These are the leaders we see in the modern GOP. These politicians are rightfully called "RINOs" (Republicans in Name Only). And I believe President Trump when he says he now wishes to devote the full measure of his life to preserving this last best hope for man on earth.

And it is precisely because the political legislative leaders of our time stand on shifting foundations, that we must recognize the genius of our Founders in establishing a government to hold true to our Founding Principles and ideals, which are reflected in the Constitution. And if we are to endure as a Constitutional republic, we must do more than recognize our government, we must insist it stand firm on the solid foundations of America, which presidents since George Washington have proclaimed are the Constitution and the Holy Bible.

It is time to re-ect President Trump, and elect legislators and judges who champion a return to traditional family values and common sense! The alternative is a further erosion of the foundations upon which this country was built. And that alternative is simply unacceptable! Why not base our fundamental core curriculum in grade schools back to the 3 Rs and the C, that is, Reading, [W]riting, [A]rithmatic, and [Good] Citizenship? And then reinforce those concepts throughout life? They served us well during the Greatest Generation and years before. Are we now too sophisticated, too technologically advanced a people to build a bridge of honor and integrity back to the fundamental values that made us a superpower and the moral example to the world in the 20th Century? I pray not!

We have much to learn from the honor and traditions of the past, and those legions that came before us. And history is replete with the downfall of nations who thought themselves infinitely wiser than their predecessors and Almighty God. The Tower of Babel and Sodom and Gomorrah immediately come to mind. God and country—I have dedicated my life to both.

During my own time as a youth, I recall a simple recitation we had in grade school following the morning prayer. It was written about America and set to music in 1831 by Samuel F. Smith. It has always served me well, and gave me pause to reflect on the past and my duty in the present. And it went exactly like this:

My country 'tis of thee, Sweet land of liberty, Of thee I sing; Land where my fathers died, Land of the pilgrim's pride, From every mountain side, Let freedom ring... Our fathers' God to thee, Author of liberty, To thee we sing. Long may our land be bright, With freedom's holy light, Protect us by they might, Great God, our King.

So, in this day and age, when good is called evil and evil good, men who embrace our Founding Principles and quest to make America great again are called homophobic, Islamophobic, or worse, let us stand in the gap for America. I am old enough to recall the same epitaphs being hurled at Ronald Reagan in 1980 when he chose as an outsider to stand against the establishment and make America great again!

There is no better time to be alive in America! Let this brief shining moment count. Let it be said of us that we were not just marking time, but that we made a difference.

Americans are not a perfect people, but we are called to a perfect mission.

I thank God that my life has been spent in a land of liberty, and that he has given me a heart to love my country with the affection of a son.

~ President Andrew Jackson

Chapter 4

Education and History

Freedom is never more than one generation away from extinction. We didn't pass it to our children in the bloodstream. It must be fought for, protected, and handed on for them to do the same, or one day we will spend our sunset years telling our children and our children's children what it was once like in the United States where men were free.

~ President Ronald Reagan

I will start this chapter with an observation: Despite eight uninterrupted years of achieving every goal on their agenda, The Obama-Biden administration and its allies on the Left in America is still in a state of outrage! And that rage is most visible in the unprecedented attack upon the Constitutional institutions of the Executive and the Judiciary. Hillary Clinton, the loser of the 2016 and standard-bearer of the Obama agenda, is actively encouraging Joe Biden not to concede the

2020 Election, should be lose. So much for her assertions in 2016 that questioning the outcome of a presidential election would be "un-American!" And so much for the Democrat Party's adherence to the time-honored peaceful transition of political power in America.

Barack Hussein Obama had success at every turn. Whether on ObamaCare, homosexual "marriage," increasing the minimum wage, increasing the national debt, enriching and empowering the fanatical Muslims in Iran and elsewhere, Obama received virtually no opposition from the Republican-led Congress or the Supreme Court. The high Court even violated its duty under the Constitution to support Obama's Left-wing radical plan to socialize America's healthcare system.

But despite victory after victory, more Americans became unemployed, less people had access to adequate, affordable healthcare coverage, more people on food stamps and government assistance, and America's borders less secure and the economy under more debt than ever before. Obama's victories were at the expense of America's livelihood and Constitutional integrity. He instituted the philosophy of his Socialist heroes and his anti-American pastor under the guise of "Hope and Change," and the end result was bringing America to the brink of extinction as a global superpower and great force for good.

To our south, we see the economic despair and desperation of Venezuela. A once thriving oil-rich economy was reduced to a testament to Socialist policies. But despite this, Socialist pockets in America elect Left-wing zealots who ignorantly champion Socialism as the pathway to prosperity. They seek to redistribute wealth by taxing hard-working Americans to satisfy their supporters, many of whom are illegals who they actually encourage to vote, in violation of the law. And those who once cried for "tolerance" for their deviant views are now the most intolerant. And what happens to these Socialist wannabes if society fails to bend to their every whim? Well, they protest, of course, violently, and double down on the bankrupt policies they champion. They, like the community organizers they worship, cry "racism" and demand even more radical change. These children of Obama and the new Democrat Party want even more in taxes taken from American taxpayers to fund their foolishness. They even turn on the radical professors that taught them such anarchy and disrespect. They reap what they have sown.

We see the violent protests of these fascists as they seek to thwart the Movement to Make America Great Again. They seek to eliminate our law enforcement community. They are the purveyors of anarchy.

America's college campuses are in chaos because of a numerical minority that aims to get their way, by force if necessary, and it has cascaded down through America's educational system. We are now raising a generation of idiots who know no better, because they were never taught properly in the first place. America must get back on track with extoling the virtues of a quality education, hard work, patriotism, Godliness, and selfless service!

And we need a Judicial system worthy of the challenges before us, not judges and justices willing to bend established law to meet the changing winds of public opinion. The Law is an anchor for stability and order in our society, and, as presidents since our Founding Father have proclaimed, the Constitution and the Bible are proper standards that form the foundation of our republic.

Teaching for me has always been a source of enjoyment. The opportunity to directly affect the educational development of fellow Americans is an awesome responsibility, and it is one I have never taken lightly.

I began to formally teach college courses as an adjunct instructor with Central Texas College in 1984. At the time, I was an active duty Army officer, teaching on a part-time, evening basis. I taught American History and Government. Two subjects I have had a profound interest in since my youth. American History and Government—these two subjects have been much maligned in recent years. The latter for good cause, especially with the advent of the Clinton, Bush and Obama administrations of government-forced Common Core curriculum that has effectively re-written American history.

Why not base our fundamental core curriculum in grade schools back to the "3 Rs" and the "C," that is, Reading, [W]riting, [A]rithmatic, and [Good] Citizenship, as I stated earlier? And then reinforce those concepts throughout life? They served us well during the Greatest Generation and years before. It worked for them and propelled America to societal and technological heights only dreamed of by mankind.

All too often, true American history, such as the significance of the Declaration of Independence and the Constitution, and with them men of character and integrity like Washington and Lee, and the impact they had on the shaping of the republic, have been erased from our children's history books and replaced with a politically correct philosophy that elevates men and women of questionable character and deeds. These are some of the Obama "achievements" I observed earlier. We have replaced truth with opinion. Combine that with the wholesale vilification of our Founding Fathers, the Ten Commandments, and the Constitution in this new-age Common Core curriculum, and we wonder what has gone wrong with America's youth?

Obama used his Bully Pulpit to lead the charge to incite violence and contempt for our members of the law enforcement community. Not mincing words here, even the mayor of Baltimore [and Secretary of the DNC] during the Obama-era encouraged and empowered rioters in the Spring of 2015; as she shared with the press, "we also gave those who wished to destroy space to do that as well."[8] What kind of examples have we set for our nation's children?

---

[8] Baltimore, MD, April 24, 2015 - Baltimore Mayor Stephanie Rawlings-Blake held a press conference to comment on the riots in honor of Freddie Gray, a citizen of Baltimore with a long criminal history. When a reporter asked her how Baltimore police would respond, she said she instructed the police officers to allow rioters to express themselves and that "we also gave those who wished to destroy space to do that as well."

Obama's legacy continues in the lawless rioters, looters and anarchists of the "Antifa" and Marxist "BLM" movements.

Thankfully, President Trump has opposed that foolishness and lawlessness. His is a Movement that respects the Rule of Law and those who enforce it! But there is resistance to this.

My frustration with the state of affairs in the world of academia began in my college years in the latter part of the 70's. The radical student protestors of the Vietnam War era in the 60's seemed to take refuge in the colleges and universities across America. For many of them, their college deferments kept them out of the war, and permanently out of the real world. Many became tenured professors in those schools and went on to foment their philosophies in the classrooms. Many never hid the fact that they loathed capitalism, the military, the police, and any semblance of authority. They were the flower children of the 60's, and they took great pleasure in their new platforms to protest the American establishment, that is, traditional family values, hard work, traditions of honor, and faith in God and country.

I never accepted the liberal, politically correct philosophy they espoused, and I took exception in the form of debate. In high school, I was a member of the Debate Team and learned to look at both sides of an issue before I took a side and argued based on the merits. My outspokenness rooted in facts and reason often cost me in the form of grades. In the world of academics, at least in some circles, innuendo and emotion were the order of the day. All in all, I was better for the experience, and learned without a doubt that one must be willing to understand the cause they support, and take a stand when it is challenged. I have learned to respect many points of view that are not necessarily my own, as long as they can be argued with facts and reason.

My experience as a professor in Massachusetts was particularly eye opening. That period started in the fall of 1987. I was just assigned by the Army to serve a tour of duty as an R.O.T.C. instructor. Specifically, I served as an Assistance Professor of Military Science at the University of Massachusetts in Amherst. I also taught R.O.T.C. classes at Western New England College in Springfield, Massachusetts. We had many fine students, but they were few and far between. The overwhelming student populations had apparently bought into the Liberal mentality that presumed anything that had to do with the military was bad. The Liberals were intolerant and bigoted, which is what they called others who disagreed with their narrow points of view. They were the products of the overwhelmingly Liberal faculty members that "educated" them.

I recall many occasions during that two-year assignment, which seemed like an eternity, when several professors of higher education liberally displayed utter contempt for American values and traditions, and, of course, the military, especially the U.S. Army.

I vividly recall on one occasion writing then-Secretary of Education William Bennett to voice my concern about the state of affairs on that campus. The Secretary was prompt and gracious in his response, reminding me very much of the man who obviously had a great influence on his life, President Reagan.

What was the Secretary's response? Be patient. Stay focused on the important things. Be an example for others to emulate. Don't be discouraged. And continue to fight the good fight. Give 'em hell! Words to live by. And so they were. And I did!

Thanks to the intervention of friends in the form of Lt. Col. Michael Hodson, from my earlier days at Fort Benning, and Maj. Gen. Robert Wagner, whom I had met at Fort Bragg, my tour of duty in what we called "the Peoples' Republic of Massachusetts" was cut short to just two years, and I was off to an assignment as an instructor on the General's Staff at Fort Monroe, Virginia, on the magnificent Chesapeake Bay. My experience in Massachusetts made me appreciate a bumper sticker I once saw on a car along Interstate 95 on the Massachusetts-New Hampshire border. It read, "Live Free or Live in Massachusetts." That about sums it up. I have always had a soft spot in my heart for the State of New Hampshire and its citizens. What patriotic American couldn't help but love a state whose motto is "Live Free or Die"?

In later years, I would teach for a number of other institutions that took pride in the part they played in meeting America's higher education needs. I taught a wide variety of classes at the undergraduate and graduate levels, including Ethics in Business and Government, Decision Analysis, International Business, and Quantitative Methods. I found teaching as an adjunct Professor of Law at Florida Coastal

School of Law in Jacksonville, Florida, particularly rewarding, both personally and professionally. Florida Coastal at the time was one of the newest ABA-accredited law schools in America, possessing a diverse and distinguished faculty committed to an imperative of civility that fosters sound decision-making on the basis of informed and reasoned judgment. I respect that!

But alas, as we have recently seen in the State of Missouri, a university president was forced to resign over allegations and threats by a small but vocal minority over unsubstantiated complaints, aided and abetted by Liberal instructors and coaches. So much for the Constitutional notions of due process and the presumption of innocence. One instructor on the University of Missouri campus, an employee of the state no less, prohibited the freedom of the press and threatened mob violence against a student reporter. Not enough that this instructor was violating the Constitution or the rules of a civil society, this mob got their way. The inmates are running the asylums on many of America's college campuses. And they will reap what they sow.

In the interim, we should demand our representatives stop taxpayer funding of institutions like the University of Missouri and others that not only condone but enable the Marxist "Black Lives Matter" crowd to disrupt these campuses and our communities, and interfere with the students who actually attend classes and want to make something of their lives. Defund these so-called "schools" of taxpayer funding, and see how fast the Liberal instructors and community organizers wither on the vine.

Conservative Americans need to reassert themselves in these Liberal hotbeds that were once designed to train America's future leaders. After all, it is the taxes taken from our hard-earned money that funds these places and provides the government-backed loans for these "students." No students who conduct themselves like the "students" we have seen on the Missouri campus should be receiving taxpayer funding in any way, shape or form!

Throughout my adult life, I have always thought it important to participate in higher education. To challenge minds to excel and think "outside the box," and build a better nation for it. To share knowledge with others and, in the process, become a more learned person myself. There is a value to sharing real world experiences and a philosophy born of reason. God knows the youth of America get enough of the other side. I like to think of it as a fair and balanced education.

Even in my campaign for Justice on the Supreme Court of Georgia, my campaign was met by intolerant voices that sought to prohibit my freedom of speech or even allow me to debate the issues of our time. And these intolerant voices included so-called "Social Justice Warrior" who were ignorant of the very rights that allowed them to spew their hate.

This was my unedited response to one such attack voiced to a local television anchor, Jim Wallace of WALB News, in Albany, Georgia, who had the decency to allow me to respond, for which I am grateful:

Dear Mr. Wallace,

Thank you for reaching out to me a short time ago to respond to allegations levelled at me. I appreciate you giving me this opportunity. My response is as follows:

When the words of any person over a lifetime are taken out of context, I realize they can be warped to fit any narrative. And I understand that politics is no place for the weak of heart or those sensitive to criticism.

I have taught United States history and the law, and have written about the same. They comprise dozens of books and countless articles over several decades. But some detractors of mine have taken words I have written in books and mixed them with fictitious social media postings to form what are anathema to my beliefs as an American and a Christian. And in that same context, I am informed that my detractors who take quotes out of context on historical figures I have written about, failed to mention any of my writings on people like Abraham Lincoln, Theodore Roosevelt, John F. Kennedy or those who penned the Constitution or served with distinction in our military.

So there is no doubt, I love the Constitution and the inalienable rights it espouses, such as the freedom of speech and the proposition of equal justice under the law, regardless of someone's race, gender, national origin or any of the immutable characteristics they may possess. In fact, I fought for those very rights as a soldier in the Army for the first 21 years of my adult life. And I have always aspired to conduct myself as a public figure in the highest traditions of the law and my upbringing. I am not perfect, but nor am I what others who do not know me would suggest I am.

But perhaps the most disheartening thing is that anyone would attempt to assassinate a candidate on the eve of an election for words in the public domain, not only taking them out of context, but actually mixing them with outright falsehoods about my service to our community and malicious fictitious tweets that I have previously disavowed as not being mine. But I realize this is politics, and some would choose to silence me because I chose to exercise my rights as an American citizen and support a presidential candidate in

2016 who some find abhorrent, but nevertheless serves as our president. And on that same token, I would never attempt to silence or discredit someone who held the opposite political beliefs, because, after all, this is America, where civil discussion and challenging points of view are a fundamental part of our lives and intellectual growth.

I am consoled by the fact that my reputation is best evidenced by the people I have encountered and work with and who know me for the person I am, not what someone who is a stranger to me and my values would tell others I am.

And to make it perfectly clear, as I have stated and will continue to state: politics and personal opinions have no business in a court of law or on the highest court in our state. My pledge is to decide matters based on the facts of each particular case and the applicable law. I will be respectful, fair and impartial. Nothing more and nothing less. That is what I have done and what I will continue to do, regardless of the outcome of this political and identifiably non-partisan race.

Thank you for the opportunity to respond.

At your service,

Hal Moroz

I often comment to friends that the young Liberal idiots we see today will eventually grow up, have responsibilities, pay taxes, and become Conservatives. But that seems less and less likely with the Democrat Party actively cultivating a base that is totally dependent on public welfare for their existence. Some call this the "Plantation," precisely because it makes its recipients dependent on their political masters, in this case the Democrat Party. This new poverty class in America will loyally support the candidate who promises the most government handouts. We have seen this in the popularity of Socialist Bernie Sanders, Hillary Clinton and now Joe Biden.

2 Thessalonians 3:10 states, "Now we command you, brethren, in the name of our Lord Jesus Christ, that ye withdraw yourselves from every brother that walketh disorderly, and not after the tradition which he received of us." Such Holy Scripture was universally embraced by our Founding Fathers!

In the words of Thomas Jefferson, "The democracy will cease to exist when you take away from those who are willing to work and give to those who would not."

It is little wonder why Jefferson and the rest of our Founders are hated by the Left. Obama dedicated his presidency, and Hillary Clinton her political life, and Joe Biden his chances of victory, to eradicating the memory of these men and their Christian Founding Principles.

The perpetrators of this political correctness that once cried for "tolerance," especially when it came to demands that we accept homosexual lifestyles as "natural," now expect the rest of America to abandon their religious convictions and Constitutional rights. We see this in the violent riots and looting in Seattle and Portland, the ridiculous homosexual "wedding cake" stories, where many in that movement are not content with obtaining these extra-societal "rights," they now want the traditional values to yield to their perversions. They demand the expulsion of God and the Holy Bible from our nation's classrooms, and, among other things, the acceptance and federal funding of the abortionists and baby part sellers. Annual taxpayer funding of the abortion industry is approaching $1 billion. This is an unconstitutional "taking" against American taxpayers.

The level of depravity on the part of the Left is sometimes hard to fathom, especially with its prevalence. They advocate so-called "art" that depicts the Cross of Christ in a jar of urine, while at the same time demanding punishment for anyone who would exercise their freedom of speech by drawing a picture of, or criticizing, the so-called "Prophet" of Islam. And if the latter was done at any institution of higher learning, you can bet anyone exercising such a freedom would be summarily dismissed, and the entire school population would undergo hours of so-called "sensitivity" training, which is more like Liberal indoctrination.

Nevertheless, those same Liberal thought police demand the silencing of any reference to the one true God, prayer, law and order, and traditional family values. Where is their call for tolerance now? Their hypocrisy is crystal clear and undeniably evident. This premeditated attack on America from within is most alarming, and it brings home the meaning of the words uttered by a dear friend in years gone by, the late William E. Simon, our former Secretary of the Treasury during the Nixon and Ford Administrations, when he said:

> On the eve of World War I, Sir Edward Grey, the British foreign secretary, issued a somber and prophetic warning. "The Lamps are going out," he said, "all over Europe." That statement could be repeated now, with one important, chilling difference. The lamps are going out, not

simply on one continent, but all over the world…They are even in danger of going out in the United States — where the torch of liberty is supposed to burn its brightest.

I believe we were placed here at this moment in America's history to keep the torch of liberty burning bright, and to preserve and strengthen this last best hope for man on earth.

I believe that those of us who are able to share wisdom with our youth have a duty to do so. To neglect that duty exposes them to the pervasive and politically correct philosophy of the mainstream media, their teachers, and the Liberal politicians.

I am often blessed by individuals who ask me to share such wisdom, and I was honored by the pastor of a local church to share my thoughts about America in an address to Camden County High School's graduating Class of 2001. I was asked to be the Guest Speaker at the high school's baccalaureate ceremony, and it was an offer that I was more than happy to accept. I share this decade and a half old speech with you to demonstrate that some principles and values are never out of style … and people long to hear the Truth!

Remarks of the Honorable H.R. "Hal" Moroz,
Camden County High School Class of 2001
Baccalaureate Ceremony, First Baptist Church
of St. Marys, Georgia, May 22nd, 2001

Ladies and gentlemen, distinguished honorees, friends, let me first say what an honor it is for me to be here with you tonight. I am humbled to stand before you. I believe this is a unique moment in our Nation's history, and a great time of opportunity.

Honored graduates, you have accomplished much, and I know I speak for all the good citizens of this county when I say, Congratulations, and Well Done! Tonight, you stand in the spotlight, and I would like to ask all gathered to recognize your achievement with a round of applause.

Would you join me? I would also like to recognize the ladies and gentlemen who supported tonight's graduates: The mothers, fathers, guardians, friends and relatives who made this event possible. So, too, would I like to recognize Pastor Keith Harwood [Pastor, First Baptist Church of St. Marys, Georgia] and Pastor Bob Moon [Pastor, Kingsland First United Methodist Church of Kingsland, Georgia]. Brother Keith and Brother Moon have a difficult task, as do all of our ministers of the Gospel. They stand in the gap for our communities. They boldly proclaim the truth, and they suffer the consequences for it.

My friends, it is not easy to take a stand, you make friends, but I dare say you make more enemies. Doing what's right is rarely easy, but it is something we are called to do. You and I. President Theodore Roosevelt once said, "Most people dwell in the Grey Twilight, which knows neither victory nor defeat."

Think about how true that is. I have heard it said that there are three kinds of people in the world. People who are oblivious to what goes on around them; People who hear about things that happen; And people who make things happen. Which one are you?

When Brother Keith first approached me about addressing you tonight, I thought, well, I can start off with a joke or other humorous line, and then get down to business. What I finally decided to do was not waste your time or the time of others in this audience. Time is precious, especially if you have a great deal to do. On the other hand, if you dwell in the Grey Twilight, time is really unimportant.

I believe you and I have a great deal to do, especially in the days and years ahead.

Tonight, I believe I am speaking to someone in this audience who may very well be a future President of the United States, a future pastor, a future legislator, judge, law enforcement officer, teacher, business leader, mother, father—you name it, each of whom has it within him or herself to change the course of American history for the better. How can I do that?—You might ask. How can one person make a difference in today's world?

226 years ago, Paul Revere entered the town of Lexington. It was around midnight. He had a message for the American people. An enemy was on the horizon: "The British are coming!" Later that morning, he was followed into town by 700 British soldiers. Regulars of the finest army the world had ever known to that point. They were met by 70 citizen-soldiers on the common. They were ordinary citizens, much like you and I. "Here once the embattled farmers stood," Emerson wrote, "and fired the shot heard round the world." They changed the course of American history!

Do you hear a call to action? A voice that cries out in the wilderness? Calling you to stand in the gap? Do you see things wrong in your lives, in our communities, in our state, and in our country? How will you answer that call? Will you close your eyes and ears to the evils of this day, and dwell in the Grey Twilight? I pray not!

Friends, we live in an interesting world. A politically correct world that tells us right is wrong and wrong is right. A world turned upside down, a world without absolutes, a world where anything goes, and you see it reflected on television, in our communities, and, yes, even in our government. You bear witness to that.

Last week, while he was being interviewed on the Fox News Network, CBS news anchorman Dan Rather said, I believe you can be honest and lie with great frequency (liberally paraphrasing his reference to former-President Clinton's integrity). Excuse me?

Two weeks ago, a New York school banned Mother's Day because it was thought to offend homosexual couples. What happened to tolerance in America? Do we now only tolerate Politically Correct ideas? What's next? Do we ban Memorial Day because it might offend anti-military activists? Do we ban 4th of July celebrations because it might offend those around the world who hate America and you and I because of what we stand for? Do we ban Labor Day because it might offend people on welfare? How about Thanksgiving and Christmas? Surely the concept of giving thanks to God and the name Jesus Christ offends people. When does the insanity end? And who among you would dare to draw a line, and say to those supporting this chaos, "Stop!"

As if that wasn't enough, today, we are told the only thing that separates us from a frog in a pond or a fish in the ocean is a hundred million years of evolution. I don't believe that! And I never will! Neither do I believe that you and I are here tonight by chance. I believe it was our destiny to be here! I believe that God in His own good pleasure had you and I here tonight for a purpose. I also believe it is not by mere chance that you and I are Americans. I also believe, as President Ronald Reagan believed, that America is separated from the rest of the world by two great oceans for a purpose! A fortress of hope in a lost world. I serve a God of order and purpose, who, despite what the Washington Post or The New York Times might say, is alive and well and has a plan for you!

I make no apologies for my admiration of President Ronald Reagan. I first met President Reagan in 1980, and one statement he made has been embedded in my mind ever since. He said, "With all the creative energy at our command, let us renew our faith and our hope—we have every right to dream heroic dreams." And so it is. President Reagan also said, "You and I have a rendezvous with destiny." And so we have.

My friends, I've read if you could shrink the earth's population down to 100 people, you would find: 57 would be Asians, 21 Europeans, 14 from North and South America, and 8 Africans; 52 would be female, 48 would be male; 70 would be non-Christian, 30 would be Christians; 80 would live in substandard housing, 70 would be unable to read, 50 would suffer from malnutrition; 6 people would possess 59% of the world's wealth, and all 6 would be from the United States; And only 1 would have a college education. With that in mind, you and I are minorities in this world. In fact, we are a privileged super-minority! Much has been given to you, my friends, and I refuse to believe it was by mere chance. God intended it to be that way! The Bible says, "to whom much is given, much is expected." Much is expected of us.

Tonight, I step out of the Grey Twilight, and into the Sunshine! Will you join me?

Be careful! I warn you! When you take a stand for righteousness, when you stand in the gap, you risk making enemies. You also risk defeat, but you chance the opportunity for victory!

Last November 7th, my wife, Denise, and I voted at Mary Lee Clark Elementary school, here in St. Marys. We arrived to vote around 6:30pm, and waited on line until 8:45pm to finally vote. We were privileged to vote, and we did! Never did it cross my mind that hours later I would be called upon to become involved in the most controversial and historic election in our lifetimes, but I was.

I was asked to serve as a Presidential Ballot inspector in the State of Florida's recount process. I recognized there would be risks involved in supporting the Constitution and the candidate of my choice. "You can make enemies doing that," I was told!

In Florida, the Constitution of the United States was a topic of debate. I heard many, who should have known better, openly say, "It's out of date!" "It's a piece of paper holding 18th Century values—we're in the 21st Century for crying out loud!"

Make no mistake, my friends, the truth is: The Constitution is as important today as it ever was! President George Washington once said, "The cornerstones of our republic are the Bible and the Constitution." He was right, and the words of our Founding Father ring true today! You see, when you have nothing as a foundation, you are liable to fall for anything!

To those of you interested in a fair and balanced, behind the scenes look at post-election Florida, I commend to you a new book by Bill Sammon, titled, *At Any Cost*. I met Mr. Salmon in Florida, while he was a reporter for *The Washington Times*. He was amazed that those of us supporting the Bush candidacy were fighting for all military absentee ballots to be counted. Yes all! Even those who voted for Mr. Gore. Why? Because it was the right thing to do.

We should support our military personnel who dwell on the very edge of freedom's domain. They protect our liberties and our way of life. Mr. Sammon's book may open your eyes to many of the shenanigans by our friends on the left—acts that included ways to reject all legal election ballots cast by active duty military personnel. Again, the title is At Any Cost. I encourage you to read it!

Months after the election was finally decided, I overheard someone at the Courthouse say, "By what right did Bush become president?" And from a distance, I heard my friend, Chief Judge Harvey Fry say, "By the Constitution!" My friends, he was right!

Chief Magistrate Harvey Fry [Chief Magistrate, Camden County, Georgia]—when he asked me to serve with him on the Court,

Judge Fry told me there were two requirements to doing the job well: Obey the Law and use common sense!

Now when have you heard advice like that in government? Obey the Law and use common sense! It sounds revolutionary today, doesn't it? You and I are privileged to have that man's hand at the reigns when it comes to the administration of justice in our county. Do you agree? If so, let him know, and remember him when you cast your vote in the next election.

All of you honored here tonight will be old enough to do that by then. My friends, I challenge you to take a stand! Do what's right! Support people doing the right things, and oppose that which is evil. Take a step out of that Grey Twilight, and walk in the Sunshine!

How can I do that? By being a good citizen! Being good students, parents, teachers, law enforcement personnel, good workers—using your God-given talents to their maximum potential. Be that kind of person God intended you to be! Make great things happen! Never lose sight of right and wrong, and be not afraid to take a stand! President Andrew Jackson said, "One man of courage makes a majority." He was right!

Some here tonight might be thinking, Judge, that's easy for you to say! You're a judge, you're a lawyer. You can take a stand! It's no big deal if you lose! My friends, for the record, I grew up in poverty. My father died a month before President Kennedy was assassinated in 1963. Life was tough. You see, no one in my family ever completed college. Most did not graduate high school! I often heard from those in my community say that people like us were not meant to go to college. Maybe you have people like that in your community.

Well, as for me, I didn't believe those people, this is America! Where else could the son of a World War II Navy combat veteran, who grew up in poverty, dream great dreams and pursue them with any degree of success? The answer is simple: Only in America!

I count my blessings every day, and I always draw upon the words on an old chaplain I met during my many years of military service. He said, "trust in God, believe in yourself, and dare to dream!" You can do anything if you have faith! I often tell people interested in going to law school, "look, if I can do it, anyone can!" And so it is.

Here, tonight, you and I have the opportunity to commit ourselves to a great Quest. To change

America for the better, and we can start by committing to improve ourselves for the better! Make us proud! Be the stuff of history! Make America a better place because of the positive influence you have on the people you meet and the institutions you touch! Some call such a Quest following the Great Commission. And so it is!

My friends, I believe that when the first chapters of the history books opening the 21st Century are written, they will read: There once was a time in our Nation's history when men and women of courage, starting in this tiny hamlet in southern Georgia, stood in the gap for America, and in what would have been the final days of our republic, changed the course of American history. You can do that! Let it be said of us that we mastered our moment, that we held tight to the reigns of America's destiny, and we refused to settle for anything less than what our God-given talents could achieve.

But I also said leaving the comfort of the Grey Twilight runs the risk of defeat. And if we should fail, let future generations read of us: There once was a time in America's history when men and women of courage, took a stand for righteousness sake, and in the final days of our republic, never gave up the fight! My friends, we must never give up the fight!

Thank you for the honor of being here with you tonight. You make me proud to be an American! God bless each of you, and God bless America! Thank you!

What ever happened to Education in America? And what about the idea that patriotism and civility are actually good for our society? We have removed morality and God from our nation's classrooms, and we wonder why our classrooms are in such utter shambles!

The question is: When does the insanity stop?

The answer is twofold: (1) When responsible parents return to being involved in the education of their children, instead of some socialist bureaucrats in Washington; and (2) when we elect statesmen who will stop appointing champions of moral relativism and political correctness to elected office and, particularly, the Judiciary.

This is another reason why I wholeheartedly support the agenda of President Trump and our Secretary of Education, Betsy DeVos. Both have set a bold vision for America's future that respects the foundation laid by our Founding Fathers. They understand the importance of the Constitution and an educational system that champions American values. They see an America that is exceptional and ready to be made great again!

The American people overwhelming reject the specious arguments of those who wish to expel God and prayers from our nation's schools and public forums. But for these judges who give life to these Liberal notions that are diametrically opposed to our traditional values and heritage, we would be far better off. In the name of political correctness we have effectively undermined, and continue to undermine, those foundations which made this country great.

So, now more than ever, this is the time to support our President and those who will reverse the disastrous course America is on, and make our country great again! After all, we are Americans, and It's Morning in America! And as President Trump said in his address to the Republican National Convention on August 27, 2020, "This is the most important election in the history of our country!"

Enter ye in at the strait gate: for wide is the gate, and broad is the way, that leadeth to destruction, and many there be which go in thereat:

Because strait is the gate, and narrow is the way, which leadeth unto life, and few there be that find it.

~ Matthew 7:13-14

Chapter 5

Profiles in Courage

One man of courage makes a majority.

~ President Andrew Jackson

Most people dwell in the Grey Twilight, which knows neither victory nor defeat. It is not the critic who counts, not the man who points out how the strong man stumbled or where the doer of deeds could have done better. The credit belongs to the man who is actually in the arena; whose face is marred by dust and sweat and blood; who strives valiantly; who errs and comes short again and again...who knows the great enthusiasm, the great devotions, and spends himself in a worthy cause; who at the least knows in the end the triumph of high achievement; and who, at the worst, if he fails, at least fails while doing greatly, so that his place shall never be with those cold and timid souls who know neither victory nor defeat.

~ President Theodore Roosevelt

Our Founding Fathers, despite what revisionist, politically correct historians may spout, were heroes, worthy of emulation, and I often think of them and their courage, especially during times of personal trial.

In that same tradition, no profile of courage would be complete if it failed to include our military and the law enforcement officers and firefighters. These are the men and women who provide the very blanket of freedom and security that allows us to live our lives as God intended. And many of these brave souls braved crumbling twin towers to rescue thousands of fellow-citizens in their time of need. They most genuinely reflect the words of Christ, when He said, "No man hath greater love than to lay down his life for a friend." Those policemen and firefighters, like the brave souls aboard the civilian jetliner that thwarted the hijacking attempt over the Pennsylvania countryside, a flight that may very well have targeted the White House or the Capitol on that fateful day of September 11, 2001, are truly American heroes. So too are the brave young Americans who answered the call to duty following the heinous attacks of the Muslim fanatics. They continue a tradition of service sparked by our Founding Fathers that has spanned wars in the desert, distant jungles, foreign shores, and here in our own homeland during the War Between the States and the Revolution.

As a youngster, and most certainly during our nation's Bicentennial Celebration, I often wondered what happened to the 56 men who signed the Declaration of Independence. My curiosity led to a dedicated research effort that revealed truly exceptional profiles of courage. These are profiles that we can all draw strength from. They are examples of great and enduring courage. They signed and they pledged their lives, their fortunes, and their sacred honour to a cause, an ideal that men had dreamed of for thousands of years. They forged a Declaration of Independence, which set forth the establishment of a nation apart from the Crown, through a revolution the likes of which was never seen in the history of man.

And true to their words, five signers of the Declaration of Independence were captured by the British as traitors, and tortured before they died. Nine of the 56 fought and died from wounds or hardships suffered during the Revolutionary War. Twelve had their homes ransacked and burned. Two lost their sons serving in the Continental Army, and two had sons captured.

But who were the Founding Fathers? Twenty-four were lawyers and judges. Twelve were wealthy colonists of varied successful backgrounds. Eleven were merchants, and nine were farmers and large plantation owners. These were men of means, well educated, and they signed the Declaration of Independence knowing full well that the penalty would be death if they were captured. Carter Braxton of Virginia, a wealthy plantation owner and trader, saw his ships swept from the seas by the British Navy. He sold his home and properties to pay his debts, and he died a pauper. The British constantly pursued Thomas McKean of Delaware. His family lived as nomads during the Revolution, moving from one location to another, and always under cover of darkness and secrecy. He served in the Congress without pay, and his family was kept in hiding. His possessions were eventually taken from him, and poverty was his reward. Tories and British soldiers looted the properties of Ellery, Hall, Clymer, Walton, Gwinnett, Heyward, Rutledge, and Middleton. At the Battle of Yorktown, Thomas Nelson, Jr., noted that British General Cornwallis had taken over his family home as a headquarters. He quietly but firmly urged General George Washington to open fire on his home. The home was destroyed, and Nelson eventually died bankrupt. Francis Lewis of New York had his home and properties destroyed. The enemy jailed his wife, and she died within a few months. John Hart of New Jersey was driven from his wife's bedside as she was dying. Their 13 children fled for their lives. His fields and his gristmill were laid to waste. For more than a year, he lived in forests and caves, returning home to find his wife dead and his children vanished. A few weeks later he died from exhaustion and a broken heart. Morris and Livingston, also from New Jersey, suffered similar fates. Such were the stories and sacrifices of the American Revolution. These were not selfish exploiters or opportunistic slave owners. They were soft-spoken men of means and education. They had security, but they valued liberty and their God-given rights more, and they were willing to step out of the Grey Twilight, and take a stand for future generations of Americans.

Make no mistake, the men who set their signatures to the Declaration of Independence understood that if things went wrong they would see their lives conclude most likely at the end of a rope on a scaffold. They were not profiteers seeking to expand their wealth. On the contrary, they were well educated, God-fearing freedom fighters, who knew no colony in the history of the British Empire ever declared its independence and successfully severed its ties with the Crown. More likely than not, their cause would fail, but these men chose death over a life without liberty. And the next time you look at a copy of the original Declaration of Independence, note John Hancock's signature. He signed his name extra-large, so that King George III could read it even without his spectacles. These men where truly profiles of courage!

Our Founding Fathers inspire me, and make me proud to be an American! It is my hope that after reading this book, you too will be inspired to develop a new sense of pride in our country and the principles it was founded on, and act accordingly.

The impact of our Founders echoes throughout the American landscape today, and I would be remiss if I did not acknowledge the ongoing work of friends like Donna Fiducia[9] and Don Neuen,[10] and Audrey Russo,[11] who like Paul Revere,

---

[9] Donna Fiducia is a former anchor of Fox News Channel, NBC, CBS Radio, VH1, and current President of Donna Fiducia Productions and co-host of the Cowboy Logic Radio Show.

[10] Don Neuen is a businessman and the co-host of the Cowboy Logic Radio Show.

[11] Audrey Russo is the Host of the REEL Talk Radio Show, a columnist and radio commentator.

sound the alarm against the forces of Political Correctness that are destroying our republic. They champion a return to the original intent of our Founding Fathers. And the selfless community work of spiritual leaders like Paul and Vickie Hafer. As the founders and leaders of the ministry staff at Lighthouse Christian Broadcasting, Paul and Vickie champion a Christian ministry ("The Lighthouse" WECC 89.3 FM, St. Marys, Georgia, serving northeast Florida & southeast Georgia, & the world on the internet at TheLighthouseFM.org,) that shines His light on southeast Georgia and northeast Florida with a simple message of Truth and Life, providing the peace of Christ that surpasses all understanding. And they are not alone. Their ministry is part of a spiritual revival that can be found in hamlets throughout our great land. I have seen such revivals in lowly homes across America, where two or more are gathered in His name. They are the salt and light of our communities.

And I have witnessed great throngs in meeting places led by champions like the late Dr. Jerry Falwell in Virginia, who actually started a Law School to train Christian lawyers and judges on our Founding Legal Principles, and Dr. Charles Stanley in Atlanta. These are the same kind of decent, God-loving citizens who filled the gap and provided Christian charity and brotherly love long before the federal and state governments ever dreamed of stepping in with their bloated welfare programs and affirmative action bureaucracies. Unlike the government programs, these ministers of the Gospel nourish the body and the soul, providing substance and meaning to life, not just a handout for living. Nevertheless, these people, by and large, are scorned by the politically correct crowd for their upright walk in life and strict adherence to the literal word of the Good Book. Their courage is self-evident! And they deserve our respect and they need our support!

We meet profiles of courage every day. They walk among us. They work with us, and they work for us, and we work for them. You just have to know where to look! Many work in homes across America, mothers raising decent children despite great personal and financial hardship. Fathers working two jobs to provide a better future for their children. I have even found them in the practice of law. Some of these profiles of courage we will never see, because they walk lonely posts in far off lands on the very edge of freedom's domain. They are the men and women serving in our military, and they watch over us 24 hours a day!

These modern-day profiles of courage are the progeny of those who gave birth to a nation, and an idea men had only dreamed of for thousands of years. I started this chapter with a tribute to our Founding Fathers, and I will end it that way.

We have a duty to reclaim our Constitution and re-establish a government worthy of their sacrifices. Voting for President Trump and those focused on restoring the Constitution and making America great again with constitute a substantial step toward that end!

The leadership of men like Madison gave shape to a nation that would become the greatest the world has ever seen. Our Founding Fathers began the most exciting adventure in the history of nations. Their victory was to find a home for liberty.

~ President Ronald Reagan

The Author's campaign for Justice on the Supreme Court of Georgia, 2020
446,026 Georgians officially cast their votes for Hal Moroz

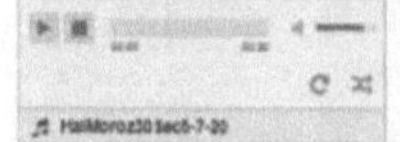

EXPERIENCE * COMMON SENSE * JUSTICE

My name is Hal Moroz, and I am running for Justice on the Supreme Court of Georgia. I would like to introduce myself to you and tell you why I care about the future of our courts in the Great State of Georgia!

I served more than 20 years in the United States military. Later, I served the good citizens of our state as both a County Judge and as a City Chief Judge in Georgia. As a Deputy Chief Assistant District Attorney, I successfully prosecuted criminals in one of Georgia's toughest jurisdictions. I have also represented military veterans in courts up to and including the United States Supreme Court. Everything about my life has been SERVICE to a cause greater than self.

I am running for this office to further serve my fellow citizens as a Justice on Georgia's highest court, and to reclaim the foundations upon which our great state and country were founded. I support the Constitution as written and a return to common sense in our judiciary. My campaign is based on three foundations … Experience, Common Sense, and Justice.

Experience * Common Sense * Justice *

* Experience: Citizens deserve Supreme Court Justices with broad experience in life and the law. My Experience in life and the law differentiates me from my opponent, more than anything else. I have served both as a prosecuting attorney and a judge. I have been a soldier and a teacher, and have the experience that reflects the diversity of the citizens of our communities, including those like myself who have held careers in the military, in my case the United States Army where my home was Fort Benning.

* Common Sense: Highlighting and Integrating the Rights of Victims in our courtrooms, and revisiting notions like trial court judges acting as a "13th juror" to nullify the guilty verdicts of juries in criminal cases is a priority of mine. These types of actions always favor the defendants, and never side with the State, the victims, or the other constitutionally recognized jurors. Trial court judges should respect the verdicts of our juries.

* Justice: I believe all judges must hold strict adherence to the Constitution and laws as written, never substituting the will of the judge for what the law actually says. This is my priority. Judicial activism is wrong. Lawmaking is the constitutional responsibility of the legislature, not the judiciary.

God willing, WITH YOUR VOTE ON THE JUNE 9 ELECTION, I will win this race for Georgia's Families and the Rule of Law!

Isn't it time for Georgia to Experience Common Sense Justice?

I ASK FOR YOUR SUPPORT TO MAKE THIS HAPPEN!

****

CAMPAIGN RADIO SPOT

THE MAKING OF A SUPREME COURT JUSTICE

The Author's campaign website (MorozLaw.com) for Justice on the Supreme Court of Georgia, 2020

The Author's campaign and an endorsement for
Justice on the Supreme Court of Georgia, 2020

https://www.gwinnettforum.com/2020/05/endorsement-issue/

Non-partisan judicial candidates

For the Georgia Supreme Court

Justice of the Supreme Court (Warren seat): For this position, we urge the election of the challenger, **H.R. Moroz**, 61, of Albany, to unseat the current judge, Sarah Warren, 38, of Atlanta. She was appointed to the high court by Gov. Nathan Deal in 2018. We base our endorsement on Mr. Moroz's long experience. He is a prosecutor in the Albany District Attorney's office, and practiced previously in Gwinnett. He is also a retired Infantry lieutenant colonel. We feel Ms. Warren lacks sufficient experience and time as an attorney to sit in the higher court.

Moroz

The Author in the service of his country as a
U.S. Army Airborne Infantry officer *(photos courtesy U.S. Army)*

Above: Author & family (Denise, son William, & daughter Heather) with friend Dr. Jerry Falwell, 1993.
Below: Author declaring his candidacy for Maryland's 5th Congressional District seat in the U.S. House of Representatives, 1993
(photo courtesy The Calvert Recorder)

Above: Author with then-House Minority Leader Newt Gingrich, R-GA,
Sep. 1993 *(Photo courtesy U.S. House of Representatives)*
Below: Author is sworn in as a Judge in the State of Georgia, Dec. 2000
(photo courtesy Camden County, GA)

Above: ADA Hal Moroz speaks to press following the conviction of a murderer he prosecuted in the State of Georgia (*Photo courtesy WALB*)
Below: Hal Moroz with Jay Sekulow, Counsel to Donald Trump

Judge Hal Moroz speaks on the 10 Commandments as the foundation of America's civil and criminal codes at WECC The Lighthouse, St. Marys, Georgia, 2004 (*Photo courtesy Paul Hafer*)

During my youth there were many wonderful sayings, now considered trite, that provided cryptic, yet prescient guidance for my life. Among them was one based on Luke 12:48: "To whom much is given of him much is required." Perhaps such sentiments are embarrassing in sophisticated company today, but I continue to believe this with all my heart. I do believe that we are required to wade into those things that matter to our country and our culture, no matter what the disincentives are, and no matter the personal cost. There is not one among us who wants to be set upon, or obligated to do and say difficult things. Yet, there is not one of us who could in good conscience stand by and watch a loved one or a defenseless person—or a vital national principle—perish alone, undefended, when our intervention could make all the difference. This may well be too dramatic an example. But nevertheless, put most simply: if we think that something is dreadfully wrong, then someone has to do something.

~ Justice Clarence Thomas, February 2001

Chapter 6

The Declaration of Independence

July 4, 1776

IN CONGRESS, July 4, 1776.

The unanimous Declaration of the thirteen united States of America,

When in the Course of human events, it becomes necessary for one people to dissolve the political bands which have connected them with another, and to assume among the powers of the earth, the separate and equal station to which the Laws of Nature and of Nature's God entitle them, a decent respect to the opinions of mankind requires that they should declare the causes which impel them to the separation.

We hold these truths to be self-evident, that all men are created equal, that they are endowed by their Creator with certain unalienable Rights, that among these are Life, Liberty and the pursuit of Happiness.--That to secure these rights, Governments are instituted among Men, deriving their just powers from the consent of the governed, --That whenever any Form of Government becomes destructive of these ends, it is the Right of the People to alter or to abolish it, and to institute new Government, laying its foundation on such principles and organizing its powers in such form, as to them shall seem most likely to effect their Safety and Happiness. Prudence, indeed, will dictate that Governments long established should not be changed for light and transient causes; and accordingly all experience hath shewn, that mankind are more disposed to suffer, while evils are sufferable, than to right themselves by abolishing the forms to which they are accustomed. But when a long train of abuses and usurpations, pursuing invariably the same Object evinces a design to reduce them under absolute Despotism, it is their right, it is their duty, to throw off such Government, and to provide new Guards for their future security.--Such has been the patient sufferance of these Colonies; and such is now the necessity which constrains them to alter their former Systems of Government. The history of the present King of Great Britain is a history of repeated injuries and usurpations, all having in direct object the establishment of an absolute Tyranny over these States. To prove this, let Facts be submitted to a candid world.

He has refused his Assent to Laws, the most wholesome and necessary for the public good.

He has forbidden his Governors to pass Laws of immediate and pressing importance, unless suspended in their operation till his Assent should be obtained; and when so suspended, he has utterly neglected to attend to them.

He has refused to pass other Laws for the accommodation of large districts of people, unless those people would relinquish the right of Representation in the Legislature, a right inestimable to them and formidable to tyrants only.

He has called together legislative bodies at places unusual, uncomfortable, and distant from the depository of their public Records, for the sole purpose of fatiguing them into compliance with his measures.

He has dissolved Representative Houses repeatedly, for opposing with manly firmness his invasions on the rights of the people.

He has refused for a long time, after such dissolutions, to cause others to be elected; whereby the Legislative powers, incapable of Annihilation, have returned to the People at large for their exercise; the State remaining in the mean time exposed to all the dangers of invasion from without, and convulsions within.

He has endeavoured to prevent the population of these States; for that purpose obstructing the Laws for Naturalization of Foreigners; refusing to pass others to encourage their migrations hither, and raising the conditions of new Appropriations of Lands.

He has obstructed the Administration of Justice, by refusing his Assent to Laws for establishing Judiciary powers. He has made Judges dependent on his Will alone, for the tenure of their offices, and the amount and payment of their salaries.

He has erected a multitude of New Offices, and sent hither swarms of Officers to harrass our people, and eat out their substance.

He has kept among us, in times of peace, Standing Armies without the Consent of our legislatures.

He has affected to render the Military independent of and superior to the Civil power.

He has combined with others to subject us to a jurisdiction foreign to our constitution, and unacknowledged by our laws; giving his Assent to their Acts of pretended Legislation:

For Quartering large bodies of armed troops among us:

For protecting them, by a mock Trial, from punishment for any Murders which they should commit on the Inhabitants of these States:

For cutting off our Trade with all parts of the world: For imposing Taxes on us without our Consent: For depriving us in many cases, of the benefits of Trial by Jury:

For transporting us beyond Seas to be tried for pretended offences

For abolishing the free System of English Laws in a neighbouring Province, establishing therein an Arbitrary government, and enlarging its Boundaries so as to render it at once an example and fit instrument for introducing the same absolute rule into these Colonies:

For taking away our Charters, abolishing our most valuable Laws, and altering fundamentally the Forms of our Governments:

For suspending our own Legislatures, and declaring themselves invested with power to legislate for us in all cases whatsoever.

He has abdicated Government here, by declaring us out of his Protection and waging War against us.

He has plundered our seas, ravaged our Coasts, burnt our towns, and destroyed the lives of our people.

He is at this time transporting large Armies of foreign Mercenaries to compleat the works of death, desolation and tyranny, already begun with circumstances of Cruelty & perfidy scarcely paralleled in the most barbarous ages, and totally unworthy the Head of a civilized nation.

He has constrained our fellow Citizens taken Captive on the high Seas to bear Arms against their Country, to become the executioners of their friends and Brethren, or to fall themselves by their Hands.

He has excited domestic insurrections amongst us, and has endeavoured to bring on the inhabitants of our frontiers, the merciless Indian Savages, whose known rule of warfare, is an undistinguished destruction of all ages, sexes and conditions.

In every stage of these Oppressions We have Petitioned for Redress in the most humble terms: Our repeated Petitions have been answered only by repeated injury. A Prince whose character is thus marked by every act which may define a Tyrant, is unfit to be the ruler of a free people.

Nor have We been wanting in attentions to our British brethren. We have warned them from time to time of attempts by their legislature to extend an unwarrantable jurisdiction over us. We have reminded them of the circumstances of our emigration and settlement here. We have appealed to their native justice and magnanimity, and we have conjured them by the ties of our common kindred to disavow these usurpations, which, would inevitably interrupt our connections and correspondence. They too have been deaf to the voice of justice and of consanguinity. We must, therefore, acquiesce in the necessity, which denounces our Separation, and hold them, as we hold the rest of mankind, Enemies in War, in Peace Friends.

We, therefore, the Representatives of the united States of America, in General Congress, Assembled, appealing to the Supreme Judge of the world for the rectitude of our intentions, do, in the Name, and by Authority of the good People of these Colonies, solemnly publish and declare, That these United Colonies are, and of Right ought to be Free and Independent States; that they are Absolved from all Allegiance to the British Crown, and that all political connection between them and the State of Great Britain, is and ought to be totally dissolved; and that as Free and Independent States, they have full Power to levy War, conclude Peace, contract Alliances, establish Commerce, and to do all other Acts and Things which Independent States may of right do. And for the support of this Declaration, with a firm reliance on the protection of divine Providence, we mutually pledge to each other our Lives, our Fortunes and our sacred Honor.

Column 1
Georgia:
  Button Gwinnett
  Lyman Hall
  George Walton

Column 2
North Carolina:
  William Hooper
  Joseph Hewes
  John Penn
South Carolina:
  Edward Rutledge
  Thomas Heyward, Jr.
  Thomas Lynch, Jr.
  Arthur Middleton

Column 3
Massachusetts:

John Hancock

Maryland:
Samuel Chase
William Paca
Thomas Stone
Charles Carroll of Carrollton
Virginia:
George Wythe
Richard Henry Lee
Thomas Jefferson
Benjamin Harrison
Thomas Nelson, Jr.
Francis Lightfoot Lee

Carter Braxton

Column 4
Pennsylvania:
  Robert Morris
  Benjamin Rush
  Benjamin Franklin
  John Morton
  George Clymer
  James Smith
  George Taylor
  James Wilson
  George Ross
Delaware:
  Caesar Rodney
  George Read
  Thomas McKean

Column 5
New York:
  William Floyd
  Philip Livingston
  Francis Lewis
  Lewis Morris
New Jersey:
  Richard Stockton
  John Witherspoon
  Francis Hopkinson
  John Hart
  Abraham Clark

Column 6
New Hampshire:
  Josiah Bartlett
  William Whipple
Massachusetts:
  Samuel Adams

John Adams
Robert Treat Paine
Elbridge Gerry
Rhode Island:
Stephen Hopkins
William Ellery
Connecticut:
Roger Sherman
Samuel Huntington
William Williams
Oliver Wolcott
New Hampshire:
Matthew Thornton

We stand here on the only island of freedom that is left in the whole world. There is no place left to flee to...no place to escape to. We defend freedom here or it is gone. There is no place for us to run, only to make a stand. And if we fail, I think we face telling our children, and our children's children, what it was we found more precious than freedom. Because I am sure that someday — if we fail in this — there will be a generation that will ask.

~ President Ronald Reagan

Chapter 7

The Federalist Papers

Federalist #1
1787

To the People of the State of New York:

AFTER an unequivocal experience of the inefficiency of the subsisting federal government, you are called upon to deliberate on a new Constitution for the United States of America. The subject speaks its own importance; comprehending in its consequences nothing less than the existence of the UNION, the safety and welfare of the parts of which it is composed, the fate of an empire in many respects the most interesting in the world. It has been frequently remarked that it seems to have been reserved to the people of this country, by their conduct and example, to decide the important question, whether societies of men are really capable or not of establishing good government from reflection and choice, or whether they are forever destined to depend for their political constitutions on accident and force. If there be any truth in the remark, the crisis at which we are arrived may with propriety be regarded as the era in which that decision is to be made; and a wrong election of the part we shall act may, in this view, deserve to be considered as the general misfortune of mankind.

This idea will add the inducements of philanthropy to those of patriotism, to heighten the solicitude which all considerate and good men must feel for the event. Happy will it be if our choice should be directed by a judicious estimate of our true interests, unperplexed and unbiased by considerations not connected with the public good. But this is a thing more ardently to be wished than seriously to be expected. The plan offered to our deliberations affects too many particular interests, innovates upon too many local institutions, not to involve in its discussion a variety of objects foreign to its merits, and of views, passions and prejudices little favorable to the discovery of truth.

Among the most formidable of the obstacles which the new Constitution will have to encounter may readily be distinguished the obvious interest of a certain class of men in every State to resist all changes which may hazard a diminution of the power, emolument, and consequence of the offices they hold under the State establishments; and the perverted ambition of another class of men, who will either hope to aggrandize themselves by the confusions of their country, or will flatter themselves with fairer prospects of elevation from the subdivision of the empire into several partial confederacies than from its union under one government.

It is not, however, my design to dwell upon observations of this nature. I am well aware that it would be disingenuous to resolve indiscriminately the opposition of any set of men (merely because their situations might subject them to suspicion) into interested or ambitious views. Candor will oblige us to admit that even such men may be actuated by upright intentions; and it cannot be doubted that much of the opposition which has made its appearance, or may hereafter make its appearance, will spring from sources, blameless at least, if not respectable--the honest errors of minds led astray by preconceived jealousies and fears. So numerous indeed and so powerful are the causes which serve to give a false bias to the judgment, that we, upon many occasions, see wise and good men on the wrong as well as on the right side of questions of the first magnitude to society. This circumstance, if duly attended to, would furnish a lesson of moderation to those who are ever so much persuaded of their being in the right in any controversy. And a further reason for caution, in this respect, might be drawn from the reflection that we are not always sure that those who advocate the truth are influenced by purer principles than their antagonists. Ambition, avarice, personal animosity, party opposition, and many other motives not more laudable than these, are apt to operate as well upon those who support as those who oppose the right side of a question. Were there not even these inducements to moderation, nothing could be more ill-judged than that intolerant spirit which has, at all times, characterized political parties. For in politics, as in religion, it is equally absurd to aim at making proselytes by fire and sword. Heresies in either can rarely be cured by persecution.

And yet, however just these sentiments will be allowed to be, we have already sufficient indications that it will happen in this as in all former cases of great national discussion. A torrent of angry and malignant passions will be let loose. To judge from the conduct of the opposite parties, we shall be led to conclude that they will mutually hope to evince the justness of their opinions, and to increase the number of their converts by the loudness of their declamations and the bitterness of their invectives. An enlightened zeal for the energy and efficiency of government will be stigmatized as the offspring of a temper fond of despotic power and hostile to the principles of liberty. An over-scrupulous jealousy of danger to the rights of the people, which is more commonly the fault of the head than of the heart, will be represented as mere pretense and artifice, the stale bait for popularity at the expense of the public good. It will be forgotten, on the one hand, that jealousy is the usual concomitant of love, and that the noble enthusiasm of liberty is apt to be infected with a spirit of narrow and illiberal distrust. On the other hand, it will be equally forgotten that the vigor of government is essential to the security of liberty; that, in the contemplation of a sound and well-informed judgment, their interest can never be separated; and that a dangerous ambition more often lurks behind the specious mask of zeal for the rights of the people than under the forbidden appearance of zeal for the firmness and efficiency of government. History will teach us that the former has been found a much more certain road to the introduction of despotism than the latter, and that of those men who have overturned the liberties of republics, the greatest number have begun their career by paying an obsequious court to the people; commencing demagogues, and ending tyrants.

In the course of the preceding observations, I have had an eye, my fellow-citizens, to putting you upon your guard against all attempts, from whatever quarter, to influence your decision in a matter of the utmost moment to your welfare, by any impressions other than those which may result from the evidence of truth. You will, no doubt, at the same time, have collected from the general scope of them, that they proceed from a source not unfriendly to the new Constitution. Yes, my countrymen, I own to you that, after having given it an attentive consideration, I am clearly of opinion it is your interest to adopt it. I am convinced that this is the safest course for your liberty, your dignity, and your happiness. I affect not reserves which I do not feel. I will not amuse you with an appearance of deliberation when I have decided. I frankly acknowledge to you my convictions, and I will freely lay before you the reasons on which they are founded. The consciousness of good intentions disdains ambiguity. I shall not, however, multiply professions on this head. My motives must remain in the depository of my own breast. My arguments will be open to all, and may be judged of by all.

They shall at least be offered in a spirit which will not disgrace the cause of truth.

I propose, in a series of papers, to discuss the following interesting particulars:

THE UTILITY OF THE UNION TO YOUR POLITICAL PROSPERITY THE INSUFFICIENCY OF THE PRESENT CONFEDERATION TO PRESERVE THAT UNION THE NECESSITY OF A GOVERNMENT AT LEAST EQUALLY ENERGETIC WITH THE ONE PROPOSED, TO THE ATTAINMENT OF THIS OBJECT THE CONFORMITY OF THE PROPOSED CONSTITUTION TO THE TRUE PRINCIPLES OF REPUBLICAN GOVERNMENT ITS ANALOGY TO YOUR OWN STATE CONSTITUTION and lastly, THE ADDITIONAL SECURITY WHICH ITS ADOPTION WILL AFFORD TO THE PRESERVATION OF THAT SPECIES OF GOVERNMENT, TO LIBERTY, AND TO PROPERTY.

In the progress of this discussion I shall endeavor to give a satisfactory answer to all the objections which shall have made their appearance, that may seem to have any claim to your attention.

It may perhaps be thought superfluous to offer arguments to prove the utility of the UNION, a point, no doubt, deeply engraved on the hearts of the great body of the people in every State, and one, which it may be imagined, has no adversaries. But the fact is, that we already hear it whispered in the private circles of those who oppose the new Constitution, that the thirteen States are of too great extent for any general system, and that we must of necessity resort to separate confederacies of distinct portions of the whole. This doctrine will, in all probability, be gradually propagated, till it has votaries enough to countenance an open avowal of it. For nothing can be more evident, to those who are able to take an enlarged view of the subject, than the alternative of an adoption of the new Constitution or a dismemberment of the Union. It will therefore be of use to begin by examining the advantages of that Union, the certain evils, and the probable dangers, to which every State will be exposed from its dissolution. This shall accordingly constitute the subject of my next address.

PUBLIUS.

Standing, as it were in the midst of falling empires, it should be our aim to assume a station and attitude, which will preserve us from being overwhelmed in their ruins.

~ President George Washington,
To the Secretary of War, December 13, 1798

NOTE: The Federalist Papers, numbering 85 in all, comprised a series of essays by Founding Fathers Alexander Hamilton, John Jay, and James Madison, first published between 1787 and 1788; they argue the need to adopt a new Constitution to replace the Articles of Confederation. Many scholars consider them divinely inspired, as they contain such prophetic warnings about the dangers inherent in an overreaching executive, legislative, and judicial branch of the federal government. They outline the limitations of government, and the subordination of the government to the constitutional protections afforded the people it represents. In particular, Federalist #78 warns against Judicial Activism by stating, *"The courts must declare the sense of the law; and if they should be disposed to exercise WILL instead of JUDGMENT, the consequence would equally be the substitution of their pleasure to that of the legislative body."* This chapter contains the text of the Federalist Paper #1, which is a General Introduction to the entire body of papers and the propositions they contain.

Readers are encouraged to research all 85 Federalist Papers in another forum, at their leisure. ~ Judge Hal Moroz

Chapter 8

The Constitution

September 17, 1787

(Preamble)

We the People of the United States, in Order to form a more perfect Union, establish Justice, insure domestic Tranquility, provide for the common defence, promote the general Welfare, and secure the Blessings of Liberty to ourselves and our Posterity, do ordain and establish this Constitution for the United States of America.

Article I (Article 1 - Legislative)

Section 1

All legislative Powers herein granted shall be vested in a Congress of the United States, which shall consist of a Senate and House of Representatives.

Section 2

1: The House of Representatives shall be composed of Members chosen every second Year by the People of the several States, and the Electors in each State shall have the Qualifications requisite for Electors of the most numerous Branch of the State Legislature.

2: No Person shall be a Representative who shall not have attained to the Age of twenty five Years, and been seven Years a Citizen of the United States, and who shall not, when elected, be an Inhabitant of that State in which he shall be chosen.

3: Representatives and direct Taxes shall be apportioned among the several States which may be included within this Union, according to their respective Numbers, which shall be determined by adding to the whole Number of free Persons, including those bound to Service for a Term of Years, and excluding Indians not taxed, three fifths of all other Persons. The actual Enumeration shall be made within three Years after the first Meeting of the Congress of the United States, and within every subsequent Term of ten Years, in such Manner as they shall by Law direct. The Number of Representatives shall not exceed one for every thirty Thousand, but each State shall have at Least one Representative; and until such enumeration shall be made, the State of New Hampshire shall be entitled to chuse three, Massachusetts eight, Rhode-Island and Providence Plantations one, Connecticut five, New-York six, New Jersey four, Pennsylvania eight, Delaware one, Maryland six, Virginia ten, North Carolina five, South Carolina five, and Georgia three.

4: When vacancies happen in the Representation from any State, the Executive Authority thereof shall issue Writs of Election to fill such Vacancies.

5: The House of Representatives shall chuse their Speaker and other Officers; and shall have the sole Power of Impeachment.

Section 3

1: The Senate of the United States shall be composed of two Senators from each State, chosen by the Legislature thereof,[3] for six Years; and each Senator shall have one Vote.

2: Immediately after they shall be assembled in Consequence of the first Election, they shall be divided as equally as may be into three Classes. The Seats of the Senators of the first Class shall be vacated at the Expiration of the second Year, of the second Class at the Expiration of the fourth Year, and of the third Class at the Expiration of the sixth Year, so that one third may be chosen every second Year; and if Vacancies happen by Resignation, or otherwise, during the Recess of the Legislature of any State, the Executive thereof may make temporary Appointments until the next Meeting of the Legislature, which shall then fill such Vacancies.

3: No Person shall be a Senator who shall not have attained to the Age of thirty Years, and been nine Years a Citizen of the

United States, and who shall not, when elected, be an Inhabitant of that State for which he shall be chosen.

4: The Vice President of the United States shall be President of the Senate, but shall have no Vote, unless they be equally divided.

5: The Senate shall chuse their other Officers, and also a President pro tempore, in the Absence of the Vice President, or when he shall exercise the Office of President of the United States.

6: The Senate shall have the sole Power to try all Impeachments. When sitting for that Purpose, they shall be on Oath or Affirmation. When the President of the United States is tried, the Chief Justice shall preside: And no Person shall be convicted without the Concurrence of two thirds of the Members present.

7: Judgment in Cases of impeachment shall not extend further than to removal from Office, and disqualification to hold and enjoy any Office of honor, Trust or Profit under the United States: but the Party convicted shall nevertheless be liable and subject to Indictment, Trial, Judgment and Punishment, according to Law.

Section 4

1: The Times, Places and Manner of holding Elections for Senators and Representatives, shall be prescribed in each State by the Legislature thereof; but the Congress may at any time by Law make or alter such Regulations, except as to the Places of chusing Senators.

2: The Congress shall assemble at least once in every Year, and such Meeting shall be on the first Monday in December,[5] unless they shall by Law appoint a different Day.

Section 5

1: Each House shall be the Judge of the Elections, Returns and Qualifications of its own Members, and a Majority of each shall constitute a Quorum to do Business; but a smaller Number may adjourn from day to day, and may be authorized to compel the Attendance of absent Members, in such Manner, and under such Penalties as each House may provide.

2: Each House may determine the Rules of its Proceedings, punish its Members for disorderly Behaviour, and, with the Concurrence of two thirds, expel a Member.

3: Each House shall keep a Journal of its Proceedings, and from time to time publish the same, excepting such Parts as may in their Judgment require Secrecy; and the Yeas and Nays of the Members of either House on any question shall, at the Desire of one fifth of those Present, be entered on the Journal.

4: Neither House, during the Session of Congress, shall, without the Consent of the other, adjourn for more than three days, nor to any other Place than that in which the two Houses shall be sitting.

Section 6

1: The Senators and Representatives shall receive a Compensation for their Services, to be ascertained by Law, and paid out of the Treasury of the United States.[6] They shall in all Cases, except Treason, Felony and Breach of the Peace, be privileged from Arrest during their Attendance at the Session of their respective Houses, and in going to and returning from the same; and for any Speech or Debate in either House, they shall not be questioned in any other Place.

2: No Senator or Representative shall, during the Time for which he was elected, be appointed to any civil Office under the Authority of the United States, which shall have been created, or the Emoluments whereof shall have been encreased during such time; and no Person holding any Office under the United States, shall be a Member of either House during his Continuance in Office.

Section 7

1: All Bills for raising Revenue shall originate in the House of Representatives; but the Senate may propose or concur with Amendments as on other Bills.

2: Every Bill which shall have passed the House of Representatives and the Senate, shall, before it become a Law, be presented to the President of the United States; If he approve he shall sign it, but if not he shall return it, with his Objections to that House in which it shall have originated, who shall enter the Objections at large on their Journal, and proceed to reconsider it. If after such Reconsideration two thirds of that House shall agree to pass the Bill, it shall be sent, together with the Objections, to the other House, by which it shall likewise be reconsidered, and if approved by two thirds of that House, it shall become a Law. But in all such Cases the Votes of both Houses shall be determined by yeas and Nays, and the Names of the Persons voting for and against the Bill shall be entered on the Journal of each House respectively. If any Bill shall not be returned by the President within ten Days (Sundays excepted) after it shall have been presented to him, the Same shall be a Law, in like Manner as if he had signed it, unless the Congress by their Adjournment prevent its Return, in which Case it shall not be a Law.

3: Every Order, Resolution, or Vote to which the Concurrence of the Senate and House of Representatives may be necessary (except on a question of Adjournment) shall be presented to the President of the United States; and before the Same shall take Effect, shall be approved by him, or being disapproved by him, shall be repassed by two thirds of the Senate and House of Representatives, according to the Rules and Limitations prescribed in the Case of a Bill.

Section 8

1: The Congress shall have Power To lay and collect Taxes, Duties, Imposts and Excises, to pay the Debts and provide for the common Defence and general Welfare of the United States; but all Duties, Imposts and Excises shall be uniform throughout the United States;

2: To borrow Money on the credit of the United States;

3: To regulate Commerce with foreign Nations, and among the several States, and with the Indian Tribes;

4: To establish an uniform Rule of Naturalization, and uniform Laws on the subject of Bankruptcies throughout the United States;

5: To coin Money, regulate the Value thereof, and of foreign Coin, and fix the Standard of Weights and Measures;

6: To provide for the Punishment of counterfeiting the Securities and current Coin of the United States;

7: To establish Post Offices and post Roads;

8: To promote the Progress of Science and useful Arts, by securing for limited Times to Authors and Inventors the exclusive Right to their respective Writings and Discoveries;

9: To constitute Tribunals inferior to the supreme Court;

10: To define and punish Piracies and Felonies committed on the high Seas, and Offences against the Law of Nations;

11: To declare War, grant Letters of Marque and Reprisal, and make Rules concerning Captures on Land and Water;

12: To raise and support Armies, but no Appropriation of Money to that Use shall be for a longer Term than two Years;

13: To provide and maintain a Navy;

14: To make Rules for the Government and Regulation of the land and naval Forces;

15: To provide for calling forth the Militia to execute the Laws of the Union, suppress Insurrections and repel Invasions;

16: To provide for organizing, arming, and disciplining, the Militia, and for governing such Part of them as may be employed in the Service of the United States, reserving to the States respectively, the Appointment of the Officers, and the Authority of training the Militia according to the discipline prescribed by Congress;

17: To exercise exclusive Legislation in all Cases whatsoever, over such District (not exceeding ten Miles square) as may, by Cession of particular States, and the Acceptance of Congress, become the Seat of the Government of the United States, and to exercise like Authority over all Places purchased by the Consent of the Legislature of the State in which the Same shall be, for the Erection of Forts, Magazines, Arsenals, dock-Yards, and other needful Buildings; — And

18: To make all Laws which shall be necessary and proper for carrying into Execution the foregoing Powers, and all other Powers vested by this Constitution in the Government of the United States, or in any Department or Officer thereof.

Section 9

1: The Migration or Importation of such Persons as any of the States now existing shall think proper to admit, shall not be prohibited by the Congress prior to the Year one thousand eight hundred and eight, but a Tax or duty may be imposed on such Importation, not exceeding ten dollars for each Person.

2: The Privilege of the Writ of Habeas Corpus shall not be suspended, unless when in Cases of Rebellion or Invasion the public Safety may require it.

3: No Bill of Attainder or ex post facto Law shall be passed.

4: No Capitation, or other direct, Tax shall be laid, unless in Proportion to the Census or Enumeration herein before directed to be taken.

5: No Tax or Duty shall be laid on Articles exported from any State.

6: No Preference shall be given by any Regulation of Commerce or Revenue to the Ports of one State over those of another: nor shall Vessels bound to, or from, one State, be obliged to enter, clear, or pay Duties in another.

7: No Money shall be drawn from the Treasury, but in Consequence of Appropriations made by Law; and a regular

Statement and Account of the Receipts and Expenditures of all public Money shall be published from time to time.

8: No Title of Nobility shall be granted by the United States: And no Person holding any Office of Profit or Trust under them, shall, without the Consent of the Congress, accept of any present, Emolument, Office, or Title, of any kind whatever, from any King, Prince, or foreign State.

Section 10

1: No State shall enter into any Treaty, Alliance, or Confederation; grant Letters of Marque and Reprisal; coin Money; emit Bills of Credit; make any Thing but gold and silver Coin a Tender in Payment of Debts; pass any Bill of Attainder, ex post facto Law, or Law impairing the Obligation of Contracts, or grant any Title of Nobility.

2: No State shall, without the Consent of the Congress, lay any Imposts or Duties on Imports or Exports, except what may be absolutely necessary for executing it's inspection Laws: and the net Produce of all Duties and Imposts, laid by any State on Imports or Exports, shall be for the Use of the Treasury of the United States; and all such Laws shall be subject to the Revision and Controul of the Congress.

3: No State shall, without the Consent of Congress, lay any Duty of Tonnage, keep Troops, or Ships of War in time of Peace, enter into any Agreement or Compact with another State, or with a foreign Power, or engage in War, unless actually invaded, or in such imminent Danger as will not admit of delay.

Article II (Article 2 - Executive)

Section 1

1: The executive Power shall be vested in a President of the United States of America. He shall hold his Office during the Term of four Years, and, together with the Vice President, chosen for the same Term, be elected, as follows

2: Each State shall appoint, in such Manner as the Legislature thereof may direct, a Number of Electors, equal to the whole Number of Senators and Representatives to which the State may be entitled in the Congress: but no Senator or Representative, or Person holding an Office of Trust or Profit under the United States, shall be appointed an Elector.

3: The Electors shall meet in their respective States, and vote by Ballot for two Persons, of whom one at least shall not be an Inhabitant of the same State with themselves. And they shall make a List of all the Persons voted for, and of the Number of Votes for each; which List they shall sign and certify, and transmit sealed to the Seat of the Government of the United States, directed to the President of the Senate. The President of the Senate shall, in the Presence of the Senate and House of Representatives, open all the Certificates, and the Votes shall then be counted. The Person having the greatest Number of Votes shall be the President, if such Number be a Majority of the whole Number of Electors appointed; and if there be more than one who have such Majority, and have an equal Number of Votes, then the House of Representatives shall immediately chuse by Ballot one of them for President; and if no Person have a Majority, then from the five highest on the List the said House shall in like Manner chuse the President. But in chusing the President, the Votes shall be taken by States, the Representation from each State having one Vote; A quorum for this Purpose shall consist of a Member or Members from two thirds of the States, and a Majority of all the States shall be necessary to a Choice. In every Case, after the Choice of the President, the Person having the greatest Number of Votes of the Electors shall be the Vice President. But if there should remain two or more who have equal Votes, the Senate shall chuse from them by Ballot the Vice President.

4: The Congress may determine the Time of chusing the Electors, and the Day on which they shall give their Votes; which Day shall be the same throughout the United States.

5: No Person except a natural born Citizen, or a Citizen of the United States, at the time of the Adoption of this Constitution, shall be eligible to the Office of President; neither shall any Person be eligible to that Office who shall not have attained to the Age of thirty five Years, and been fourteen Years a Resident within the United States.

6: In Case of the Removal of the President from Office, or of his Death, Resignation, or Inability to discharge the Powers and Duties of the said Office, the Same shall devolve on the VicePresident, and the Congress may by Law provide for the Case of Removal, Death, Resignation or Inability, both of the President and Vice President, declaring what Officer shall then act as President, and such Officer shall act accordingly, until the Disability be removed, or a President shall be elected.

7: The President shall, at stated Times, receive for his Services, a Compensation, which shall neither be encreased nor diminished during the Period for which he shall have been elected, and he shall not receive within that Period any other Emolument from the United States, or any of them.

8: Before he enter on the Execution of his Office, he shall take the following Oath or Affirmation: — "I do solemnly swear (or affirm) that I will faithfully execute the Office of President of the United States, and will to the best of my Ability, preserve, protect and defend the Constitution of the United States."

Section 2

1: The President shall be Commander in Chief of the Army and Navy of the United States, and of the Militia of the several States, when called into the actual Service of the United States; he may require the Opinion, in writing, of the principal Officer in each of the executive Departments, upon any Subject relating to the Duties of their respective Offices, and he shall have Power to grant Reprieves and Pardons for Offences against the United States, except in Cases of Impeachment.

2: He shall have Power, by and with the Advice and Consent of the Senate, to make Treaties, provided two thirds of the Senators present concur; and he shall nominate, and by and with the Advice and Consent of the Senate, shall appoint Ambassadors, other public Ministers and Consuls, Judges of the supreme Court, and all other Officers of the United States, whose Appointments are not herein otherwise provided for, and which shall be established by Law: but the Congress may by Law vest the Appointment of such inferior Officers, as they think proper, in the President alone, in the Courts of Law, or in the Heads of Departments.

3: The President shall have Power to fill up all Vacancies that may happen during the Recess of the Senate, by granting Commissions which shall expire at the End of their next Session.

Section 3

He shall from time to time give to the Congress Information of the State of the Union, and recommend to their Consideration such Measures as he shall judge necessary and expedient; he may, on extraordinary Occasions, convene both Houses, or either of them, and in Case of Disagreement between them, with Respect to the Time of Adjournment, he may adjourn them to such Time as he shall think proper; he shall receive Ambassadors and other public Ministers; he shall take Care that the Laws be faithfully executed, and shall Commission all the Officers of the United States.

Section 4

The President, Vice President and all civil Officers of the United States, shall be removed from Office on Impeachment for, and Conviction of, Treason, Bribery, or other high Crimes and Misdemeanors.

Article III (Article 3 - Judicial)

Section 1

The judicial Power of the United States, shall be vested in one supreme Court, and in such inferior Courts as the Congress may from time to time ordain and establish. The Judges, both of the supreme and inferior Courts, shall hold their Offices during good Behaviour, and shall, at stated Times, receive for their Services, a Compensation, which shall not be diminished during their Continuance in Office.

Section 2

1: The judicial Power shall extend to all Cases, in Law and Equity, arising under this Constitution, the Laws of the United States, and Treaties made, or which shall be made, under their Authority;—to all Cases affecting Ambassadors, other public Ministers and Consuls;—to all Cases of admiralty and maritime Jurisdiction;—to Controversies to which the United States shall be a Party;—to Controversies between two or more States;—between a State and Citizens of another State; —between Citizens of different States, —between Citizens of the same State claiming Lands under Grants of different States, and between a State, or the Citizens thereof, and foreign States, Citizens or Subjects.

2: In all Cases affecting Ambassadors, other public Ministers and Consuls, and those in which a State shall be Party, the supreme Court shall have original Jurisdiction. In all the other Cases before mentioned, the supreme Court shall have appellate Jurisdiction, both as to Law and Fact, with such Exceptions, and under such Regulations as the Congress shall make.

3: The Trial of all Crimes, except in Cases of Impeachment, shall be by Jury; and such Trial shall be held in the State where the said Crimes shall have been committed; but when not committed within any State, the Trial shall be at such Place or Places as the Congress may by Law have directed.

Section 3

1: Treason against the United States, shall consist only in levying War against them, or in adhering to their Enemies, giving them Aid and Comfort. No Person shall be convicted of

Treason unless on the Testimony of two Witnesses to the same overt Act, or on Confession in open Court.

2: The Congress shall have Power to declare the Punishment of Treason, but no Attainder of Treason shall work Corruption of Blood, or Forfeiture except during the Life of the Person attainted.

Article IV (Article 4 - States' Relations)

Section 1

Full Faith and Credit shall be given in each State to the public Acts, Records, and judicial Proceedings of every other State. And the Congress may by general Laws prescribe the Manner in which such Acts, Records and Proceedings shall be proved, and the Effect thereof.

Section 2

1: The Citizens of each State shall be entitled to all Privileges and Immunities of Citizens in the several States.

2: A Person charged in any State with Treason, Felony, or other Crime, who shall flee from Justice, and be found in another State, shall on Demand of the executive Authority of the State from which he fled, be delivered up, to be removed to the State having Jurisdiction of the Crime.

3: No Person held to Service or Labour in one State, under the Laws thereof, escaping into another, shall, in Consequence of any Law or Regulation therein, be discharged from such

Service or Labour, but shall be delivered up on Claim of the Party to whom such Service or Labour may be due.

Section 3

1: New States may be admitted by the Congress into this Union; but no new State shall be formed or erected within the Jurisdiction of any other State; nor any State be formed by the Junction of two or more States, or Parts of States, without the Consent of the Legislatures of the States concerned as well as of the Congress.

2: The Congress shall have Power to dispose of and make all needful Rules and Regulations respecting the Territory or other Property belonging to the United States; and nothing in this Constitution shall be so construed as to Prejudice any Claims of the United States, or of any particular State.

Section 4

The United States shall guarantee to every State in this Union a Republican Form of Government, and shall protect each of them against Invasion; and on Application of the Legislature, or of the Executive (when the Legislature cannot be convened) against domestic Violence.

Article V (Article 5 - Mode of Amendment)

The Congress, whenever two thirds of both Houses shall deem it necessary, shall propose **Amendments** to this Constitution, or, on the Application of the Legislatures of two thirds of the several States, shall call a Convention for proposing Amendments, which, in either Case, shall be valid to all Intents and Purposes, as Part of this Constitution, when ratified by the Legislatures of three fourths of the several States, or by Conventions in three fourths thereof, as the one or the other Mode of Ratification may be proposed by the Congress; Provided that no Amendment which may be made prior to the Year One thousand eight hundred and eight shall in any Manner affect the first and fourth Clauses in the Ninth Section of the first Article; and that no State, without its Consent, shall be deprived of its equal Suffrage in the Senate.

Article VI (Article 6 - Prior Debts, National Supremacy, Oaths of Offic)

1: All Debts contracted and Engagements entered into, before the Adoption of this Constitution, shall be as valid against the United States under this Constitution, as under the Confederation.

2: This Constitution, and the Laws of the United States which shall be made in Pursuance thereof; and all Treaties made, or which shall be made, under the Authority of the United States, shall be the supreme Law of the Land; and the Judges in every State shall be bound thereby, any Thing in the Constitution or Laws of any State to the Contrary notwithstanding.

3: The Senators and Representatives before mentioned, and the Members of the several State Legislatures, and all executive and judicial Officers, both of the United States and of the several States, shall be bound by Oath or Affirmation, to support this Constitution; but no religious Test shall ever be required as a Qualification to any Office or public Trust under the United States.

Article VII (Article 7 - Ratification)

The Ratification of the Conventions of nine States, shall be sufficient for the Establishment of this Constitution between the States so ratifying the Same.

The Word "the", being interlined between the seventh and eight Lines of the first Page, The Word "Thirty" being partly written on an Erazure in the fifteenth Line of the first Page. The Words "is tried" being interlined between the thirty second and thirty third Lines of the first Page and the Word "the" being interlined between the forty third and forty fourth Lines of the second Page.

done in Convention by the Unanimous Consent of the States present the Seventeenth Day of September in the Year of our Lord one thousand seven hundred and Eighty seven and of the Independence of the United States of America the Twelfth **In witness** whereof We have hereunto subscribed our Names,

Attest
William
Jackson
Secretary

G^o: Washington -Presid^t. and deputy from Virginia

Delaware

Geo: Read
Gunning Bedford jun
John Dickinson
Richard Bassett
Jaco: Broom

Maryland

James McHenry
Dan of S^t   Thos. Jenifer
Danl Carroll.

Virginia

John Blair —
James Madison Jr.

North Carolina

Wm Blount
Rich^d. Dobbs Spaight.
Hu Williamson

South Carolina

J. Rutledge
Charles Cotesworth Pinckney
Charles Pinckney
Pierce Butler.

Georgia

William Few
Abr Baldwin

New Hampshire

John Langdon
Nicholas Gilman

Massachusetts

Nathaniel Gorham
Rufus King

Connecticut

W^m. Saml. Johnson
Roger Sherman

New York

Alexander Hamilton

New Jersey

Wil. Livingston
David Brearley.
W^m. Paterson.
Jona: Dayton

Pennsylvania

B Franklin
Thomas Mifflin
Robt Morris
Geo. Clymer
Thos. FitzSimons
Jared Ingersoll
James Wilson.
Gouv Morris

Letter of Transmittal

In Convention. Monday September 17th 1787.

Present
The States of

New Hampshire, Massachusetts, Connecticut, Mr. Hamilton from New York, New Jersey, Pennsylvania, Delaware,

Maryland, Virginia, North Carolina, South Carolina and Georgia.

Resolved, That the preceeding Constitution be laid before the United States in Congress assembled, and that it is the Opinion of this Convention, that it should afterwards be submitted to a Convention of Delegates, chosen in each State by the People thereof, under the Recommendation of its Legislature, for their Assent and Ratification; and that each Convention assenting to, and ratifying the Same, should give Notice thereof to the United States in Congress assembled. Resolved, That it is the Opinion of this Convention, that as soon as the Conventions of nine States shall have ratified this Constitution, the United States in Congress assembled should fix a Day on which Electors should be appointed by the States which shall have ratified the same, and a Day on which the Electors should assemble to vote for the President, and the Time and Place for commencing Proceedings under this Constitution.

That after such Publication the Electors should be appointed, and the Senators and Representatives elected: That the Electors should meet on the Day fixed for the Election of the President, and should transmit their Votes certified, signed, sealed and directed, as the Constitution requires, to the Secretary of the United States in Congress assembled, that the Senators and Representatives should convene at the Time and Place assigned; that the Senators should appoint a President of the Senate, for the sole Purpose of receiving, opening and counting the Votes for President; and, that after he shall be chosen, the Congress, together with the President, should, without Delay, proceed to execute this Constitution.

By the unanimous Order of the

Convention

W. Jackson Secretary. G⁰: Washington -Presid^t.

Letter of Transmittal to the President of Congress

In Convention. Monday September 17th 1787.

SIR:

We have now the honor to submit to the consideration of the United States in Congress assembled, that Constitution which has appeared to us the most advisable.

The friends of our country have long seen and desired that the power of making war, peace, and treaties, that of levying money, and regulating commerce, and the correspondent executive and judicial authorities, should be fully and effectually vested in the General Government of the Union; but the impropriety of delegating such extensive trust to one body of men is evident: hence results the necessity of a different organization.

It is obviously impracticable in the Federal Government of these States to secure all rights of independent sovereignty to each, and yet provide for the interest and safety of all. Individuals entering into society must give up a share of liberty to preserve the rest. The magnitude of the sacrifice must depend as well on situation and circumstance, as on the object to be obtained. It is at all times difficult to draw with precision the line between those rights which must be surrendered, and those which may be preserved; and, on the present occasion, this difficulty was increased by a difference among the several States as to their situation, extent, habits, and particular interests.

In all our deliberations on this subject, we kept steadily in our view that which appears to us the greatest interest of every true American, the consolidation of our Union, in which is involved our prosperity, felicity, safety — perhaps our national existence. This important consideration, seriously and deeply impressed on our minds, led each State in the Convention to be less rigid on points of inferior magnitude than might have been otherwise expected; and thus, the Constitution which we now present is the result of a spirit of amity, and of that mutual deference and concession, which the peculiarity of our political situation rendered indispensable.

That it will meet the full and entire approbation of every State is not, perhaps, to be expected; but each will, doubtless, consider, that had her interest alone been consulted, the consequences might have been particularly disagreeable or injurious to others; that it is liable to as few exceptions as could reasonably have been expected, we hope and believe; that it may promote the lasting welfare of that Country so dear to us all, and secure her freedom and happiness, is our most ardent wish.

With great respect, we have the honor to be,

SIR, your excellency's most obedient and

humble servants:

GEORGE WASHINGTON, *President.*

By the unanimous order of the convention.

His Excellency the President of Congress.

Amendments to the Constitution

(The procedure for changing the United States Constitution is **Article V** - Mode of Amendment)

(The Preamble to The Bill of Rights)

Congress OF THE United States

begun and held at the City of New-York, on Wednesday the fourth of March, one thousand seven hundred and eighty nine.

THE Conventions of a number of the States, having at the time of their adopting the Constitution, expressed a desire, in order to prevent misconstruction or abuse of its powers, that further declaratory and restrictive clauses should be added: And as extending the ground of public confidence in the Government, will best ensure the beneficent ends of its institution.

RESOLVED by the Senate and House of Representatives of the United States of America, in Congress assembled, two thirds of both Houses concurring, that the following Articles be proposed to the Legislatures of the several States, as amendments to the Constitution of the United States, all, or any of which Articles, when ratified by three fourths of the said Legislatures, to be valid to all intents and purposes, as part of the said Constitution; viz.

ARTICLES in addition to, and Amendment of the **Constitution of the United States of America**, proposed by Congress, and ratified by the Legislatures of the several States, pursuant to the fifth Article of the original Constitution.

(Articles I through X are known as the Bill of Rights)

-

Article the first. .... After the first enumeration required by the first Article of the Constitution, there shall be one Representative for every thirty thousand, until the number shall amount to one hundred, after which, the proportion shall be so regulated by Congress, that there shall be not less than one hundred Representatives, nor less than one Representative for every forty thousand persons, until the number of Representatives shall amount to two hundred, after which the proportion shall be so regulated by Congress, that there shall not be less than two hundred Representatives, nor more than one Representative for every fifty thousand persons.

-

Article the second. .... No law, varying the compensation for the services of the Senators and Representatives, shall take effect, until an election of Representatives shall have intervened.

Article [I] (Amendment 1 - Freedom of expression and religion)

Congress shall make no law respecting an establishment of religion, or prohibiting the free exercise thereof; or abridging the freedom of speech, or of the press; or the right of the people peaceably to assemble, and to petition the Government for a redress of grievances.

Article [II] (Amendment 2 - Bearing Arms)

A well regulated Militia, being necessary to the security of a free State, the right of the people to keep and bear Arms, shall not be infringed.

Article [III] (Amendment 3 - Quartering Soldiers)

No Soldier shall, in time of peace be quartered in any house, without the consent of the Owner, nor in time of war, but in a manner to be prescribed by law.

Article [IV] (Amendment 4 - Search and Seizure)

The right of the people to be secure in their persons, houses, papers, and effects, against unreasonable searches and seizures, shall not be violated, and no Warrants shall issue, but upon probable cause, supported by Oath or affirmation, and particularly describing the place to be searched, and the persons or things to be seized.

Article [V] (Amendment 5 - Rights of Persons)

No person shall be held to answer for a capital, or otherwise infamous crime, unless on a presentment or indictment of a Grand Jury, except in cases arising in the land or naval forces, or in the Militia, when in actual service in time of War or public danger; nor shall any person be subject for the same offence to be twice put in jeopardy of life or limb; nor shall be compelled in any criminal case to be a witness against himself, nor be deprived of life, liberty, or property, without due process of law; nor shall private property be taken for public use, without just compensation.

Article [VI] (Amendment 6 - Rights of Accused in Criminal Prosecutions)

In all criminal prosecutions, the accused shall enjoy the right to a speedy and public trial, by an impartial jury of the State and district wherein the crime shall have been committed, which district shall have been previously ascertained by law, and to be informed of the nature and cause of the accusation; to be confronted with the witnesses against him; to have compulsory process for obtaining witnesses in his favor, and to have the Assistance of Counsel for his defence.

Article [VII] (Amendment 7 - Civil Trials)

In Suits at common law, where the value in controversy shall exceed twenty dollars, the right of trial by jury shall be preserved, and no fact tried by a jury, shall be otherwise re-examined in any Court of the United States, than according to the rules of the common law.

Article [VIII] (Amendment 8 - Further Guarantees in Criminal Cases)

Excessive bail shall not be required, nor excessive fines imposed, nor cruel and unusual punishments inflicted.

Article [IX] (Amendment 9 - Unenumerated Rights)

The enumeration in the **Constitution**, of certain rights, shall not be construed to deny or disparage others retained by the people.

Article [X] (Amendment 10 - Reserved Powers)

The powers not delegated to the United States by the Constitution, nor prohibited by it to the States, are reserved to the States respectively, or to the people.

Attest,
John Beckley, Clerk of the House of Representatives.
Sam. A. Otis Secretary of the Senate.

Frederick Augustus Muhlenberg Speaker of the House of Representatives.
John Adams, Vice-President of the United States, and President of the Senate.

(end of the Bill of Rights)

[Article XI] (Amendment 11 - Suits Against States)

The Judicial power of the United States shall not be construed to extend to any suit in law or equity, commenced or prosecuted against one of the United States by Citizens of another State, or by Citizens or Subjects of any Foreign State.

[Article XII] (Amendment 12 - Election of President)

The Electors shall meet in their respective states, and vote by ballot for President and Vice-President, one of whom, at least, shall not be an inhabitant of the same state with themselves; they shall name in their ballots the person voted for as President, and in distinct ballots the person voted for as Vice-President, and they shall make distinct lists of all persons voted for as President, and of all persons voted for as Vice-President, and of the number of votes for each, which lists they shall sign and certify, and transmit sealed to the seat of the government of the United States, directed to the President of the Senate;—The President of the Senate shall, in the presence of the Senate and House of Representatives, open all the certificates and the votes shall then be counted;—The person having the greatest number of votes for President, shall be the President, if such number be a majority of the whole number of Electors appointed; and if no person have such majority, then from the persons having the highest numbers not exceeding three on the list of those voted for as President, the House of Representatives shall choose immediately, by ballot, the President. But in choosing the President, the votes shall be taken by states, the representation from each state having one vote; a quorum for this purpose shall consist of a member or members from two-thirds of the states, and a majority of all the states shall be necessary to a choice. And if the House of Representatives shall not choose a President whenever the right of choice shall devolve upon them, before the fourth day of March next following, then the Vice-President shall act as President, as in the case of the death or other constitutional disability of the President. —The person having the greatest number of votes as Vice-President, shall be the Vice-President, if such number be a majority of the whole number of Electors appointed, and if no person have a majority, then from the two highest numbers on the list, the Senate shall choose the Vice-President; a quorum for the purpose shall consist of two-thirds of the whole number of Senators, and a majority of the whole number shall be necessary to a choice. But no person constitutionally ineligible to the office of President shall be eligible to that of Vice-President of the United States.

Article XIII (Amendment 13 - Slavery and Involuntary Servitude)

Neither slavery nor involuntary servitude, except as a punishment for crime whereof the party shall have been duly convicted, shall exist within the United States, or any place subject to their jurisdiction.

Congress shall have power to enforce this article by appropriate legislation.

Article XIV (Amendment 14 - Rights Guaranteed: Privileges and Immunities of Citizenship, Due Process, and Equal Protection)

1: All persons born or naturalized in the United States, and subject to the jurisdiction thereof, are citizens of the United States and of the State wherein they reside. No State shall make or enforce any law which shall abridge the privileges or immunities of citizens of the United States; nor shall any State deprive any person of life, liberty, or property, without due process of law; nor deny to any person within its jurisdiction the equal protection of the laws.

2: Representatives shall be apportioned among the several States according to their respective numbers, counting the whole number of persons in each State, excluding Indians not taxed. But when the right to vote at any election for the choice of electors for President and Vice President of the United States, Representatives in Congress, the Executive and Judicial officers of a State, or the members of the Legislature thereof, is denied to any of the male inhabitants of such State, being twenty-one years of age,[15] and citizens of the United States, or in any way abridged, except for participation in rebellion, or other crime, the basis of representation therein shall be reduced in the proportion which the number of such male citizens shall bear to the whole number of male citizens twenty-one years of age in such State.

3: No person shall be a Senator or Representative in Congress, or elector of President and Vice President, or hold any office, civil or military, under the United States, or under any State, who, having previously taken an oath, as a member of Congress, or as an officer of the United States, or as a member of any State legislature, or as an executive or judicial officer of any State, to support the Constitution of the United States, shall have engaged in insurrection or rebellion against the same, or given aid or comfort to the enemies thereof. But Congress may by a vote of two-thirds of each House, remove such disability.

4: The validity of the public debt of the United States, authorized by law, including debts incurred for payment of pensions and bounties for services in suppressing insurrection or rebellion, shall not be questioned. But neither the United States nor any State shall assume or pay any debt or obligation incurred in aid of insurrection or rebellion against the United States, or any claim for the loss or emancipation of any slave; but all such debts, obligations and claims shall be held illegal and void.

5: The Congress shall have power to enforce, by appropriate legislation, the provisions of this article.

Article XV (Amendment 15 - Rights of Citizens to Vote)

The right of citizens of the United States to vote shall not be denied or abridged by the United States or by any State on account of race, color, or previous condition of servitude.

The Congress shall have power to enforce this article by appropriate legislation.

Article XVI (Amendment 16 - Income Tax)

The Congress shall have power to lay and collect taxes on incomes, from whatever source derived, without apportionment among the several States, and without regard to any census or enumeration.

[Article XVII] (Amendment 17 - Popular Election of Senators)

1: The Senate of the United States shall be composed of two Senators from each State, elected by the people thereof, for six years; and each Senator shall have one vote. The electors in each State shall have the qualifications requisite for electors of the most numerous branch of the State legislatures.

2: When vacancies happen in the representation of any State in the Senate, the executive authority of such State shall issue writs of election to fill such vacancies: Provided, That the legislature of any State may empower the executive thereof to make temporary appointments until the people fill the vacancies by election as the legislature may direct.

3: This amendment shall not be so construed as to affect the election or term of any Senator chosen before it becomes valid as part of the Constitution.

Article [XVIII] (Amendment 18 - Prohibition of Intoxicating Liquors)

1: After one year from the ratification of this article the manufacture, sale, or transportation of intoxicating liquors within, the importation thereof into, or the exportation thereof from the United States and all territory subject to the jurisdiction thereof for beverage purposes is hereby prohibited.

2: The Congress and the several States shall have concurrent power to enforce this article by appropriate legislation.

3: This article shall be inoperative unless it shall have been ratified as an amendment to the Constitution by the legislatures of the several States, as provided in the Constitution, within seven years from the date of the submission hereof to the States by the Congress.

Article [XIX] (Amendment 19 - Women's Suffrage Rights)

The right of citizens of the United States to vote shall not be denied or abridged by the United States or by any State on account of sex.

Congress shall have power to enforce this article by appropriate legislation.

Article [XX] (Amendment 20 - Terms of President, Vice President, Members of Congress: Presidential Vacancy)

1: The terms of the President and Vice President shall end at noon on the 20th day of January, and the terms of Senators and Representatives at noon on the 3d day of January, of the years in which such terms would have ended if this article had not been ratified; and the terms of their successors shall then begin.

2: The Congress shall assemble at least once in every year, and such meeting shall begin at noon on the 3d day of January, unless they shall by law appoint a different day.

3: If, at the time fixed for the beginning of the term of the President, the President elect shall have died, the Vice President elect shall become President. If a President shall not have been chosen before the time fixed for the beginning of his term, or if the President elect shall have failed to qualify, then the Vice President elect shall act as President until a President shall have qualified; and the Congress may by law provide for the case wherein neither a President elect nor a Vice President elect shall have qualified, declaring who shall then act as President, or the manner in which one who is to act shall be selected, and such person shall act accordingly until a President or Vice President shall have qualified.

4: The Congress may by law provide for the case of the death of any of the persons from whom the House of Representatives may choose a President whenever the right of choice shall have devolved upon them, and for the case of the death of any of the persons from whom the Senate may choose a Vice President whenever the right of choice shall have devolved upon them.

5: Sections 1 and 2 shall take effect on the 15th day of October following the ratification of this article.

6: This article shall be inoperative unless it shall have been ratified as an amendment to the Constitution by the legislatures of three-fourths of the several States within seven years from the date of its submission.

Article [XXI] (Amendment 21 - Repeal of Eighteenth Amendment)

1: The eighteenth article of amendment to the Constitution of the United States is hereby repealed.

2: The transportation or importation into any State, Territory, or possession of the United States for delivery or use therein of intoxicating liquors, in violation of the laws thereof, is hereby prohibited.

3: This article shall be inoperative unless it shall have been ratified as an amendment to the Constitution by conventions in the several States, as provided in the Constitution, within seven years from the date of the submission hereof to the States by the Congress.

Amendment XXII (Amendment 22 - Presidential Tenure)

1: No person shall be elected to the office of the President more than twice, and no person who has held the office of President, or acted as President, for more than two years of a term to which some other person was elected President shall be elected to the office of the President more than once. But this article shall not apply to any person holding the office of President when this article was proposed by the Congress, and shall not prevent any person who may be holding the office of President, or acting as President, during the term within which this article becomes operative from holding the office of President or acting as President during the remainder of such term.

2: This article shall be inoperative unless it shall have been ratified as an amendment to the Constitution by the legislatures of three-fourths of the several states within seven years from the date of its submission to the states by the Congress.

Amendment XXIII (Amendment 23 - Presidential Electors for the District of Columbia)

1: The District constituting the seat of government of the United States shall appoint in such manner as the Congress may direct: A number of electors of President and Vice President equal to the whole number of Senators and Representatives in Congress to which the District would be entitled if it were a state, but in no event more than the least populous state; they shall be in addition to those appointed by the states, but they shall be considered, for the purposes of the election of President and Vice President, to be electors appointed by a state; and they shall meet in the District and perform such duties as provided by the twelfth article of amendment.

2: The Congress shall have power to enforce this article by appropriate legislation.

Amendment XXIV (Amendment 24 - Abolition of the Poll Tax Qualification in Federal Elections)

1. The right of citizens of the United States to vote in any primary or other election for President or Vice President, for electors for President or Vice President, or for Senator or

Representative in Congress, shall not be denied or abridged by the United States or any state by reason of failure to pay any poll tax or other tax.

2. The Congress shall have power to enforce this article by appropriate legislation.

Amendment XXV (Amendment 25 - Presidential Vacancy, Disability, and Inability)

1: In case of the removal of the President from office or of his death or resignation, the Vice President shall become President.

2: Whenever there is a vacancy in the office of the Vice President, the President shall nominate a Vice President who shall take office upon confirmation by a majority vote of both Houses of Congress.

3: Whenever the President transmits to the President pro tempore of the Senate and the Speaker of the House of Representatives his written declaration that he is unable to discharge the powers and duties of his office, and until he transmits to them a written declaration to the contrary, such powers and duties shall be discharged by the Vice President as Acting President.

4: Whenever the Vice President and a majority of either the principal officers of the executive departments or of such other body as Congress may by law provide, transmit to the President pro tempore of the Senate and the Speaker of the House of Representatives their written declaration that the President is unable to discharge the powers and duties of his office, the Vice President shall immediately assume the powers and duties of the office as Acting President.

Thereafter, when the President transmits to the President pro tempore of the Senate and the Speaker of the House of Representatives his written declaration that no inability exists, he shall resume the powers and duties of his office unless the Vice President and a majority of either the principal officers of the executive department or of such other body as Congress may by law provide, transmit within four days to the President pro tempore of the Senate and the Speaker of the House of Representatives their written declaration that the President is unable to discharge the powers and duties of his office. Thereupon Congress shall decide the issue, assembling within forty-eight hours for that purpose if not in session. If the Congress, within twenty-one days after receipt of the latter written declaration, or, if Congress is not in session, within twenty-one days after Congress is required to assemble, determines by two-thirds vote of both Houses that the President is unable to discharge the powers and duties of his office, the Vice President shall continue to discharge the same as Acting President; otherwise, the President shall resume the powers and duties of his office.

Amendment XXVI (Amendment 26 - Reduction of Voting Age Qualification)

1: The right of citizens of the United States, who are 18 years of age or older, to vote, shall not be denied or abridged by the United States or any state on account of age.

2: The Congress shall have the power to enforce this article by appropriate legislation.

Amendment XXVII (Amendment 27 - Congressional Pay Limitation)

No law varying the compensation for the services of the Senators and Representatives shall take effect until an election of Representatives shall have intervened.

Freedom is never more than one generation away from extinction. We didn't pass it to our children in the bloodstream. It must be fought for, protected, and handed on for them to do the same, or one day we will spend our sunset years telling our children and our children's children what it was once like in the United States where men were free.

~ President Ronald Reagan

Afterword

Let's Make America Great Again

Let us raise a standard to which the wise and honest can repair; the rest is in the hands of God.

~ President George Washington,
from his Address to the Constitutional Convention, 1787

This story shall the good man teach his son; And Crispin Crispian shall ne'er go by, From this day to the ending of the world, But we in it shall be remembered,—We few, we happy few, we band of brothers; For he to-day that sheds his blood with me Shall be my brother; be he ne'er so vile, This day shall gentle his condition: And gentlemen in England now a-bed Shall think themselves accurs'd they were not here, And hold their manhoods cheap while any speaks That fought with us upon Saint Crispin's day.

~ Shakespeare, King Henry V, Act IV, Scene III

In the waning days of the British Empire, soldiers and knights sworn to the cause, before they departed on what could have very well been their final Quest, parted company with a simple saying: "I'll see you at sundown." They, better than most, knew that a cancer was spreading throughout the empire, and the day was fast approaching when men of honor would be left alone to stand in the gap. And one fateful day, just before the end, they would stand shoulder to shoulder in a last ditch effort to stem the tide, that is, to stop the sun from setting on that once-great institution, which contributed so greatly to the culture of Western Civilization, the British Empire.

Pax Americana is over! The peace we enjoyed has been squandered by a great many politicians. And here I blame not only the Democrat and Republican establishment politicians, but I blame the members of the Judiciary as well. They have forsaken their duty under the Constitution and their oaths to God and the American people. It is now time for another generation of Americans, outsiders if you will, to enter the arena and repair the damage, and reclaim the promise of America.

But it must be understood that an end the Pax Americana is not necessarily an end to America as a world superpower and a force for good. The events that brought about an end to Greece and Rome and finally Great Britain as dominate world forces for good need not spell America's downfall. There is still time, but that precious time is dwindling.

America has many problems, but we have a great many more blessings. We have it within our power to avoid the fates that befell other great powers like Greece, Rome and Great Britain. We can change the course of American history! I believe that men and women of courage and good will can change the course of American history for the better. And in case you have any doubts, I am talking about YOU!

I believe in America! I believe God is the author of the American experience and our salvation. We are here not as the product of some evolutionary quirk of science, but as part of a great and divine plan to do good. We were perfectly placed here at this time in the history of the world to make a difference. I believe that of Donald J. Trump as well. He, like Ronald Reagan and others before him in American history, can make America great again, but he cannot do it alone! It will take the concerned efforts of men and women to join this Movement, and propel America positively into the future.

But as I alluded to earlier, even as rich and as powerful as Donald J. Trump may be, his message is infinitely greater! The power of the presidency rests not in wealth or personal power, it rests in the ability to positively influence others. That's called leadership! The President uses the Bully Pulpit to affect change by providing a vision for our citizens to rally around, and he appoints cabinet member to implement that vision, and he appoints members of the federal judiciary to uphold the strict letter of the Constitution, regardless of what the other branches of government may say, or at least that is how it is supposed to be.

I dare say President Obama did not subscribe to that Founding Principle. He used the Bully Pulpit to divide America racially, politically and economically, and he used it as a platform to incite the lowest form of inhabitants in our land to riot and wage war against our law enforcement community. He also appointed lawyers to the federal judiciary that perverted the Constitution and made their will the law. This is Obama's legacy!

Nevertheless, we can fulfil President Reagan's vision that "America's best days are yet to come!" But it bears keeping in mind that there will be trials along the way. As the Good Book, particularly the Book of Psalms, proclaims, we learn more from our valley experiences than we do at the hilltops. My friends, we have spent many years in the valley, let us rise to the occasion and march toward the top of the hill! The forces of darkness are great, but God is greater!

We must each in our own way labor to make America great again, adhering to our Christian Founding Principles, which are sown in the very fabric our Declaration of Independence and the Constitution! As Psalm 127:1 states, "Except the LORD build the house, they labour in vain that build it: except the LORD keep the city, the watchman waketh but in vain." We need to rebuild America with a healthy reverence for our Creator and respect for the rule of law. It is here that our Judiciary plays no small part. Judges and Justices are the keepers of the Law.

Remember, *Making America Great Again* requires the embodiment of the same mindset and work ethic that made

America great to begin with. Truth, Justice, a reverence to God and our country's Founding Principles, and the vision and good deeds to see them through. This includes voting for the re-election of President Trump, a Conservative-Republican Congress, and state-level champions of America's Founding Principles, whether they be governors, judges, legislators, mayors or city council members. Re-electing President Trump at the national level and electing patriots like Marjorie Taylor Greene to Congress in northwest Georgia and Rindy Howell to the St. Marys City Council at the local level in Georgia and elsewhere is what *The Cause Goes On* is all about!

Again, so there is no doubt, and as I stated at the start of this work, I lost a great many times in my life, and I have lost loved ones, but the fight goes on. And I have come to realize that failure is sometimes the first step toward success. "Lay me down and bleed awhile," Reagan said in 1976, when he lost his first bid to become President. "Though I am wounded, I am not slain." As the Great Communicator said, "I shall rise and fight again." He did!

This, my friends, is our time to rise and fight again! It is a defining moment in the history of our nation. Right here, right now, it begins — A time of great responsibility to be greatly borne. Let it be said of us that we mastered our moment, we kept what President Ronald Reagan called our "rendezvous with destiny," and we refused to let America go quietly into the night.

When the first chapter of the history books opening the 21st Century are written, let it be said of us — we happy few, we band of brothers, we last of the good knights—that we kept faith with our Founding Fathers, we stood in the gap, and, in what would have been the final days of our Republic, we never gave up the fight. We must never give up the fight!

My friends, Pax Americana is at an end. But unlike Rome and Great Britain, this does not necessarily mean the end of America's era as the preeminent force for good in the world. We have it within our power to break the cycle of history, but we must seize a vision of boldness for America's future. We can reclaim the legal and moral high ground that fueled the Great American Spirit throughout our history, we can defend America's territorial integrity, build a great wall to our south, deport those who illegally violated our borders and exist here as criminals, rebuild our military and honor the Veterans who answered their country's call, especially our wounded warriors.

Do these themes sound familiar? They should. They are part of the bold vision of one candidate who became President against the odds, Donald J. Trump. Now we must fight the good fight and win the re-election of this champion of our Christian values and the Constitution! We truly can make America great again!

This is the challenge of our time ... To take a stand for America! This is what it means to be an American, and what we are called to be. And I believe the thoughts and ideas I have articulated in this work were shared by our Founding Fathers and are still shared by the silent majority of Americans today, with implications that reach far beyond the bounds of personal self-interest.

I pray this work will be a wake-up call to the once Silent Majority, a call to action, and a source of hope and encouragement.

In 1775, Paul Revere entered the town of Lexington. It was around midnight, and he had a wake up message for the citizens: "The British are coming! The British are coming!"

The following morning, 700 British soldiers entered the town and were met by 70 citizen-soldiers on the Common. "Here once the embattled farmers stood," Emerson wrote, "and fired the shot heard round the world."

Today, we hear another call. A call to arms. We are at war on many fronts. A new kind of war against anarchists in our streets, a global Muslim caliphate, and a war to confront an unprecedented attack against our children, our economy, our military, our sovereignty, our cultural heritage, and our legal system. This is a war between the forces of good and evil for the survival of America and the last remnants of civilization. We cannot afford to lose!

If ever there was a time of need, a time for men and women of courage and good will to step forward and be counted, this is such a time. A time for you and I to stand in the gap for America and what remains of Western Civilization and the rule of law.

It is Morning Again in America under the administration of President Trump! This was no small achievement! However, it will take determination, effort, and a great resolve to re-elect our President and institutionalize the changes needed to return to our Founding Principles, but we can do it! We can make this last best hope for man on earth great again! Now that would be a very American thing to do! God willing, our goal will be achieved!

Let's Make America Great Again!

Jesus said unto him,

Thou shalt love the Lord thy God with all thy heart,
and with all thy soul, and with all thy mind.

This is the first and great commandment.

And the second is like unto it,
Thou shalt love thy neighbour as thyself.

On these two commandments hang all the law and the prophets.

~ Matthew 22:37-40

If my people, which are called by my name,
shall humble themselves, and pray, and seek my face,
and turn from their wicked ways;
then will I hear from heaven, and will forgive their sin,
and will heal their land.

~ 2 Chronicles 7:14

About the Author

Judge Hal Moroz

Whether therefore ye eat, or drink, or whatsoever ye do,
do all to the glory of God.

~ Psalm 37:23

Judge Hal Moroz was a candidate for Justice on the Supreme Court of Georgia on the June 9th, 2020 Election, which was also the Presidential Primary Election in the Great State of Georgia. Although he lost his race, Judge Moroz garnered 446,026 votes from across the state and brought national attention to the problems facing our modern judiciary.

Hal Moroz is an Attorney and Counselor at Law, who served as an Assistant District Attorney, a County Judge, and a city Chief Judge in the great State of Georgia. His practice in the law has ranged from prosecuting criminals on behalf of the State of Georgia to representing American military veterans in courts up to and including the Supreme Court of the United States.

Judge Moroz is also an accomplished soldier and statesman, as well as a retired U.S. Army officer, having served in the Airborne Infantry. Judge Moroz served on the faculty of Florida Coastal School of Law in Jacksonville, Florida, and the State Bar of Georgia's Institute for Continuing Legal Education (ICLE) in the education of attorneys. He is a former candidate for the U.S. Congress, and served as Special Counsel to the Georgia Republican Party's First Congressional District Committee in the 2000 primary and general elections.

Hal Moroz frequently serves as a news and political commentator, sharing his insight of the law and politics on a variety of popular media programs. He is also a prolific writer, having authored numerous legal articles, weekly legal newspaper columns, and books. Copies of his many books can be ordered at Amazon.com or any major bookstore!

Hal Moroz can be reached through an internet search
or through his email at: hal@morozlaw.com or his website:
MorozLaw.com

I am an American who lives in the shadow of the Cross ...

I walk humbly before God,
I stand tall before men,
And I stand in the gap for America!

~ Judge Hal Moroz